DESTINY '39

A young soldier's experiences during World War II.

John Swain

DESTINY '39

A young soldier's experiences during World War II.

John Swain

Pen Press Publishers Ltd
39-41 North Road, Islington, London N7 9DP

First Published in Great Britain in 2001
by Pen Press Publishers Limited,
39-41 North Road, Islington,
London N7 9DP

Copyright © John Swain 2001

**British Library Cataloguing-in-Publication Data.
A catalogue record for this book is available
from the British Library.**

ISBN 1 900796 73 2

All rights reserved. No part of this publication may be reproduced,
stored in a retrieval system or transmitted in any form or by any means
electric, mechanical, photocopying, recording or otherwise,
without the prior permission of the publisher.

Cover design by
Catrina Sherlock

Contents

Introduction

Part One	I Join The Army	1
	Dispatch Rider Wanted	19
	A Limber Gunner	33
	Aberporth Firing Camp	38
	Battery Fitter	43
Part Two	On The Move	49
	Fitter Course At Letchworth	50
	Gun Fitter Course At Woolwich	58
	Finsbury Park Gun Site	60
	R.A.F. Wattisham	62
	The Interview With Colonel Imrie R.C.M.P.	65
	We Move To Orkney	72
	The Military College Of Science	83
	The 2nd Infantry Brigade Workshops	88
Part Three	Overseas To North Africa	95
	Algiers	101
	Bone	104
	Teboursouk	106
	Sousse	111
	Kelibia	113
	Hammamet	118
	Meeting The French Foreign Legion	123
	Searching With An Electric Magnet	128
	An Epitaph To 'Bull'	131
	Limbo in Tunisia	135

Part Four	The Move To Italy	141
	Spinazola	143
	Fianno	145
	Anzio	148
	My Near Demise	156
	Anzio	159
	Rome	165
	Caldini	167
	The Massacre in Rome	171
	Borgo San Lorenzo	176
	The San Clemente Valley	184
	The Long Route Home	186
Part Five	The Long Route Home	189
	Camp 87 Pardes Hanna	190
	Cairo	191
	Camp 87 Pardes Hanna	193
	Geniefa	201
	The Long Route Home	203

Illustrations

Gunner Swain	9
The Government Training Centre - Letchworth - 1940	51
Lance Sergeant Swain - 1941	63
Extract from 'The Reme Journal'	152
The Victor Emmanuel Monument, Rome - 1944	169
A.Q.M.S. Swain and A.S.M. Bennet in June 1944	172
A.S.M. Swain - Borgo San Lorenzo - September 1944	180
Battery Sergeant Major Johnson and A.S.M. Swain in Cairo - 1945	194
Members of the 19th Field Regt. L.A.D., Pades Hanna - 1945	197
A group of 19th Field Regt. Sergeant's visit the Sphinx and Pyramids of Giza - 1945	198
With Battery Sergeant Major Johnson in Cairo - 1945	199

Introduction

Every young man has an ambition of some sort, often born of imagination and hero worship; but many amount to nothing in the long run. I had an ambition from a very early age, and it influenced quite strongly everything I did. I wanted to be a policeman when I grew up.

It was an ambition that sprang from the utter respect and admiration that I had for my father, the man who had brought me up firmly but fairly in those formative years. A man who had been a farm labourer, a railwayman, a gamekeeper's assistant, and a policeman in Scotland, then a soldier during the Great War. After that war, he returned to England as a drill sergeant in the Scots Guards at the Guards' Depot at Caterham in Surrey. On being demobilised, he took up employment in London as a policeman, and became a successful detective.

To help me fulfil my ambition when I left school, I took up boring work as a clerk which allowed me a little time to continue my studies with the aim of sitting the police entrance examination. Those years passed very slowly. Then, shortly after my nineteenth birthday in August, 1939, when war clouds were looming, I decided to take my own form of action. My father had been a soldier; why should I not follow in his footsteps?

I joined the local Territorial Army Regiment, the 99th London Welsh Regiment, Royal Artillery, Anti Aircraft, T.A. I enlisted as a Gunner, and was called up as soon as I joined up. It did not take me long to adjust to army life. Discipline had always been fairly strict in my family, and I was determined not to let the family tradition down.

I had learned much from my father, and was quite handy with the normal run of tools, a skill that was to stand me in very good stead. I became the Battery, Sergeant Fitter.

Destiny '39

I was successful in this field, and was later recommended to go to the Military College of Science at Stoke-on-Trent to continue my study of Field Artillery guns. I passed out as an Armament Artificer (Field) with the rank of Staff Sergeant in the Royal Army Ordnance Corps. The R.A.O.C., was soon amalgamated with the then recently formed Royal Electrical and Mechanical Engineers, and I was transferred to R.E.M.E. I served R.E.M.E. in the U.K. North Africa, Italy, Palestine, Syria, Lebanon, and Egypt. I was extremely lucky during this period and suffered only one very near miss when on the Anzio Beachhead, an experience I will never forget.

Finally, after the war, I travelled from Egypt to France, thence back to England, and demobilisation in March, 1946. There I left behind some of the proudest moments of my life that live with me to this very day. My original ambition took charge, and I joined the London Metropolitan Police, retiring in 1976 as Detective Superintendent in charge of the Scotland Yard Robbery Squad and holder of the Queens Police Medal for Distinguished Service. Not a bad life. Furthermore, I have enjoyed every minute of it.

PART ONE

I Join The Army

I have often thought of the extremely interesting, instructive, and exciting times that I experienced in the army as a young man. This was in spite or perhaps because of the fact that the bulk of my military service was in wartime. I had never planned to be a soldier, somehow it just happened.

It may sound like something of an excuse when I say that my education during my formative years was just the normal secondary school type experienced by the sons and daughters of most working class people. I did, however, attempt to increase my knowledge by attending evening classes regularly while I worked as an office clerk.

My nineteenth birthday was on 15th August, 1939, and as I got out of bed that day, I could see from my bedroom window that there were a number of soldiers in the sports ground at the back of our house. Some of them were pitching tents, others were marking out the ground for something. Then four large guns came trundling in and were placed in the centre of the field. These were obviously artillery pieces. Surely we were not expecting to be invaded? Questions flashed through my mind. As for answers, I had none. Over breakfast, my father said that they were anti-aircraft guns, and that the object of the exercise was to be prepared in case the Germans decided to bomb us. What a thought!

At work, there had been much talk of the possibility of war with Germany. Opinions on this point differed considerably. Some people seemed to think that the Germans had learned their lesson in the Great War, others that war was a very real threat. The Germans were clearly on the march in Europe, but surely they would not declare war on us again?

My father was a serving Police Officer who was making the grade as a C.I.D. Officer, and slowly climbing the ladder of promotion. He had been a soldier himself during the Great War, and had been wounded on three occasions. He brought me up strictly but fairly and in a manner that earned him my greatest respect, to the extent that my one ambition even when at school was to emulate him, and join the London Metropolitan Police when I came of age.

My biggest worry on this score was that I could never see myself passing the entrance examination. I had examined some of the civil service exam papers, which were of a similarly high standard to those set for police entrants, and it was to this end that most of my studies were directed. This included learning shorthand. Not that this subject would be part of the examination, but I wanted to assure my father that I was indeed studying and following his guidance. He had told me back in 1937 that there would in due course be a vacant position for a junior C.I.D. clerk, who could assist the officers in their paperwork.

Early in the summer of 1939, I learned that such a position was likely to be offered to young men who wanted to join the Police Force. Applicants had to be at least nineteen years of age. Furthermore, they would be required to produce a certificate to prove that they were capable of writing eighty words a minute in shorthand.

I was pleased about this, as I had proved myself at night school by taking down dictation at 120 words a minute. I could foresee no problem, and in due course put in for the required test to obtain an eighty-words-a-minute certificate.

As I recall, on 30th August, 1939 I attended my night school, full of confidence, and sat down to take the dictation. One problem

I had never experienced but often heard spoken about soon came to the fore. It is used on many occasions as an excuse (or valid reason) for failure - examination nerves. I was never a nervous person, but within a few minutes of the dictation beginning, I knew that the examiner was running away from me, and I was missing out words.

I failed the test and, bordering on broken-hearted, made my way home. At the time, we were living in a charming semi-detached house in Woodmansterne Road, Norbury, which backed on to the Westminster Bank Sports Ground. My mother opened the front door, and with a smile asked me how I had got on with the examination. I told her that I had failed. The smile went immediately, and she let rip with all manner of abuse as to my general ability. I was no good, I was useless. I would never get into the Police. In fact she could not think of any worthwhile job I would be good for.

I stood in the doorway listening to her abuse. She was probably right in the circumstances, but I had to do something to justify myself and, if possible, prove her wrong. Without answering her or saying anything, I turned and walked back towards Norbury High Street. My mind was in turmoil. As a young boy, one of the supreme punishments my mother had threatened me with when I upset her was that she would 'put' me in the army.

War clouds were definitely looming, there was no doubt about that. The Germans were extending their territorial claims in Europe. I was now approaching Norbury Police Station. I stopped and looked up at the blue lamp.

My father had been a soldier in one war; now another one was drawing near according to all of the news forecasts I had listened to. What's wrong with being a soldier? I asked myself. I was young and fit. The Territorial Army wanted volunteers, and there I would at least learn something, although at the time I had no idea what.

I walked up to the desk in the police station and asked the Sergeant if he could give me the addresses of the local Territorial Army recruiting offices. No problem. He gave me the names and addresses which I made a mental note of. There was the Royal Army Service Corps at Mitcham Road, Croydon, and the London Welsh Regiment at Mitcham Lane, Streatham.

My father had been a Sergeant in the Scots Guards during the Great War. Before that he had been an officer in the Dundee Police. As he was quite obviously a proud Scot, it did not seem right to join a Welsh regiment. I held a provisional driving licence, and had successfully driven Dad's car as a learner, under instruction; therefore the Royal Army Service Corps seemed the regiment to go for.

Where was that one now? I asked myself. Oh yes, Mitcham Lane, Streatham. I caught the bus at Hermitage Bridge, and made my way to Streatham. I had a rough idea of just where the army recruiting office would be, and walked back along Mitcham Lane. I decided to report to the Royal Army Service Corps and join up immediately. During the walk, I turned my plan over in my mind. Was this the right thing to do? Was I sure? Yes, my mind was definitely made up, and at that moment I arrived outside a large private house with a notice outside saying that it was an Army Recruiting Office.

I walked straight in. A most charming man, smart as the proverbial new pin, approached me. He was wearing the uniform of a regimental Sergeant Major, the breed of soldier that music hall jibes so often mock as loud-mouthed bullies. This man, however, was a perfect gentleman who I later learned was Regimental Sergeant Major Flemming.

'So you want to join the army, lad?' he said. 'You're just the type we're looking for - sit down son - where do you live? What's your father's nationality?'

'Scottish,' I replied.

'What nationality is your mother?' he asked.

'English,' I answered.

'Any Welsh blood?' he asked.

I should have realised my mistake there and then, but I did not. 'My mother's maiden name is Price, I believe her mother was Welsh.'

I got no further, my inquisitor extended his hand and said, 'If her name was Price and that's Welsh, you'll do.'

I was then taken into another room and introduced to an army captain. From his shoulder flash I realised that he was from the Royal Army Medical Corps. I was told that he was going to give me a medical examination; this so-called medical examination took only a few minutes, after which he announced that I was A1 in fitness. Don't ask me how he came to that conclusion. I was then returned to the regimental Sergeant Major, who was in the next room.

He in turn took me to another room, where another officer was sitting behind a desk. There, a very short ceremony, now very vague in my memory, took place. His final words, however, still ring clear: 'Congratulations, young man. You are now Gunner Swain, John E., of 303 Battery 99th London Welsh Regiment, Royal Artillery.' The reality then dawned on me. Everything had happened so fast. What had I done - a Welsh Regiment?

I was still in something of a daze when the gentleman in the Sam Browne belt tapped me on the shoulder and ushered me out of the office. I was truly shaken. 'Christ,' I said. 'I thought that this was the Royal Army Service Corps recruiting office.' There was a very sudden and marked change in the attitude of the man I had started to look upon as a friend. He stiffened, and in so doing, seemed to gain two or three inches in height. His eyes flashed in the most frightening manner that I had ever seen.

As I said to myself, God, this man has got to be an actor, he bellowed, 'You are in the London Welsh Regiment, the finest regiment in the British Army, and don't you forget it, my lad. The officer told you that you had been embodied. That means called up. There is an emergency. You will report to the Westminster

Bank Sports Ground, Norbury at 9am tomorrow morning, and don't you be late.'

I stammered something like, 'What am I going to tell my employer?' He laughed and, still in his booming voice, said, 'Tell him that the best thing he can do before he gets called up is to join up himself.'

He then ushered me out of the building, once again warning me not to be late in the morning. I walked home from Streatham, a distance of about two miles. This was obviously not my day. I had yet to tell my father of my failure in the shorthand examination. Now I had joined a Welsh regiment, and that was what worried me most as I got nearer to home.

Then a strange thing happened. I was about 100 yards from my front gate when my worries dispersed. I was now in the army, and would join my regiment the following day. That was quite final In any event, in my heart I wanted to join the army. On entering my house, I found both my mother and father anxiously awaiting my return. I knew my mother would have told my father that I had failed the shorthand examination, so there was little point in mentioning that sore point. I therefore took the bull by the horns.

'I've joined the army, Dad,' I said. 'The regiment has been called up and I have to report at nine o'clock tomorrow morning over the back here, in the sports ground.' Mother came to the rescue, doing what most mothers do when their son suddenly gets called up. She cried. Dad comforted her, and the pressure was off me. Phew, was I relieved!

I was not questioned as to why I had joined the army, in fact, the rest of the evening was spent listening to sound words of advice from my father. Words like: 'I was in the Scots Guards. Still my pride and joy. As a serving soldier, I believed it was the finest regiment in the British Army, and it's still number one in my mind. You have joined the London Welsh, and to you it must be the finest. A soldier without pride in his regiment is no use to anyone, only the enemy. Walk tall, lad. Be proud.'

As I was going to be busy in the morning, I decided to write to my employer, the Co-operative Wholesale Society, 99 Leman Street, Aldgate, London E.1. I told them that I had joined the Territorial Army and been called up.

I took some time over this letter, as it was most important to me. I tendered an apology for the fact that I would not be back at work until the existing State of Emergency was over. My main worry was that I could get the sack for not giving the approved notice. Then when I came out of the army, I would have difficulty in obtaining a reference, another position of employment, or getting into the Police Force.

The general feeling all round had been that if there was a war, it would only last for about six months, hence my personal worry; but of course, this was not to be. I retired to my bed, mulling over those words of wisdom from my father, relieved and very happy.

I woke early on 29th. August, 1939. There had been a lot of shouting in the Westminster Bank Sports Ground, and I had not slept soundly that night. After breakfast, I took my leave of the family with a lump in my throat, Mother in tears and Dad patting me on the back and saying, 'You'll be all right, son.' I then made my way to the large club-house on the other side of the sports ground.

Once inside the building I found it far removed from what I thought a club-house should look like. There I was directed to the orderly room where Sergeant Williams was in charge. The Sergeant proceeded to ask me all manner of questions which he laboriously took down in writing. I was then taken to the Quartermaster's store, a large long hut outside the club-house, and there kitted out with a uniform, service dress, brass buttons, ammunition, boots and everything. Yes, everything down to the two blankets, button stick and toothbrush. Once dressed in this new attire, I felt very proud indeed, but those bloody boots were heavy! Little did I know how I would learn to love them over the years. Then I looked again. How on earth did one ever manage to look smart in these uniforms? The stiff collar was going to make my neck sore in minutes. Oh, I had so much to learn.

There was no let-up, however. I was taken to a hut beside the Quartermaster's store, and shown an area of floor where I was to sleep when told. Then I was shown how to lay out my kit by day. Other articles of kit were neatly stacked in various parts of this hut. I stacked my kit in a similar manner, and put my civilian clothes under the neatly folded blankets. I was told that I should arrange for these items to be collected as soon as possible, for they were now no longer any use to me.

The next move was to an area in the far corner of the sports ground that had a patch of concrete laid. There I was introduced to Battery Sergeant Major Giles and four other Gunners, dressed like myself. By their mode of dress, they too seemed to have only just joined the regiment.

Clearly the Sergeant Major had done a lot of boxing in his time. He had the ears and a nose that testified to this. He proceeded to give us our first lesson in drill. His commands were perfect, delivered in a loud cockney voice, but doing what he asked was extremely difficult for us new recruits.

The Sergeant Major was, strange to say, patient with us despite our many failings, and I was beginning to wonder just how long that patience would last. Then it happened. For the umpteenth time one of our number turned left instead of right. The Sergeant Major let out a very loud yell of 'Allah, send me some soldiers!', threw his swagger cane, point first, hard on the concrete, then, placing his hands together as if in prayer, went down on one knee. The swagger cane had bounced high in the air, but our Sergeant Major, with his head still bowed and without looking up, raised his right hand in the air and caught the cane as it returned to the ground. How we all retained our calm I don't know; I for one, and I'm sure the same applied to my colleagues, nearly burst out laughing.

Gunner Swain ~ 1939

Standing erect, the picture of a very smart soldier, the Sergeant Major calmly but loudly announced: 'You lot might have had some fun with me, but before I have finished with you, you are going to be a lot of very smart soldiers that I shall be proud of.'

He could see that we were by now fairly relaxed, and he started once again: 'And you, Gunner ——, will at least know your left from your bloody right by the time I have finished with you.' He then turned smartly, ordered us to 'Quick march' and moved us off to the kitchen inside the club-house.

There we were confronted with a veritable mountain of potatoes and directed to peel them. Happily the Sergeant cook produced two potato peelers, but at the same time he calmly announced that he had purposely purchased them himself in order to prevent the likes of us turning tomorrow's dinner into a heap of peelings. I seized one of these tools and with one of the others set about peeling the potatoes. Not a bad choice actually, for I then saw that the other four recruits were confronted with the largest pile of washing up that I had ever seen.

My potato peeling came to a sudden and pleasant halt when the cook Sergeant came to us and said, 'I suppose, as you've just joined us, you might have a few bob still in your pocket. You'd better come and have a look at our canteen.' We did as bid, followed the bold Sergeant. Sure enough, the original club-house bar was being put to very good use. For my part, I had drunk very little up to that time, apart from the occasional shandy and a very rare beer. We bought the Sergeant a beer each, and had a very pleasant evening enjoying the company. Thankfully, my colleagues, who were a little older than I, did not attempt to get me to drink too much.

The evening was made all the more enjoyable by some beautiful singing. I myself have never had much of a singing voice, but these Welshmen sang beautifully. The best of all was a character I had seen working in the cookhouse, who was referred to as 'Cooky Hughes'. He sang so well he almost brought tears to my eyes.

At ten o'clock I left the canteen and returned to my kit. There I put my previous efforts at camping to good use. Soon, wrapped in my two blankets on the hut floor, I was sound asleep.

What seemed like only minutes later, the sound of the guard hammering on the door woke us. It was 6.30am, and he suggested that the six of us had better get ourselves dressed in overalls and go to the mess room for breakfast. (My colleagues were those who had been on drill instruction with me the previous day.) We therefore hurriedly washed, shaved and dressed as ordered and were soon consuming a handsome breakfast of bacon and eggs with lashings of fried tomatoes, and as much tea as we could drink.

When breakfast was over, a Lance Bombardier - Lance Corporal to the uninitiated - bellowed out in a loud voice, 'You six, follow me' and pointed to our table. We got up and followed him to one of the gun emplacements. There, we were handed picks and shovels, and began digging trenches and filling sandbags. Slowly, and while it was still light, we built a sandbag wall round the gun. This, we were told, was a 3.7-inch anti-aircraft gun which, with the aid of the other instruments grouped in the middle of the four guns, was capable of knocking the German Luftwaffe out of the sky.

Digging, guard duties, cookhouse and other fatigues came all too often, but at least there seemed to be a good reason for everything we did. Then one day, while we were building a further gun emplacement, the howling of the air-raid sirens stopped us in our work. It was 3rd. September, 1939 and, as I recall it, mid morning. It seemed that everyone had stopped whatever they were doing. Looking round, I noticed everyone looking to the skies as if expecting to see the German air force at any minute, and I was of a similar mind. There were no planes, but it was only a matter of minutes before officers and Sergeants I had never seen before appeared. We were divided into gun crews and began learning how to handle these monsters.

11

It was all very interesting. By following the directions given by the predictor and other instruments on the dials in front of the gun layers, we were told we should be able to shoot down the enemy. I had not seen one round of ammunition, but there were a number of ammunition boxes containing shells. However, there was the small matter of fusing those shells to consider, which would take up another important lesson.

The days that followed were spent doing all manner of training. Most important of all was the actual gun training. Furthermore, we were told that we were approaching the time when we would all go to Aberporth on the coast of Wales and actually fire these guns - a very necessary exercise if we were to gain confidence in their ability to do what was expected of them. I was beginning to thoroughly admire the mechanical skill which had gone into making the guns, and I was dying to learn more about them and what really made them tick.

Guard duty seemed to come round all too often, and I very soon got fed up with drinking cocoa out of a dixie in the middle of the night. Then one night while on perimeter patrol, which we carried out in pairs, I realised that we were walking past the fence at the bottom of the garden of our house in Woodmansterne Road. I looked over the fence and saw my mother and father sitting by the fireside. My colleague must have thought I was mad as I picked up a small stone and threw it at the back window. My Spaniel Mac barked his head off, and charged the back door. Then my father got up, came to the back door and opened it.

I called out quietly as I could under the circumstances. My father realised it must have been me, and came down to the fence. I explained to him that we were on perimeter patrol, and that we would like a cup of home-made tea. He told us to wait a couple of minutes and he would bring us one. Not only did he bring us tea and cakes, but he also brought with him an old walnut fishing reel that I still have to this day. With the ratchet in position it made a loud noise if turned. I had no idea what he was up to, but he was never lost for ideas.

Dad then proceeded to explain that he was going to fix the fishing reel under the mantelpiece in the back room where he had been sitting, facing the back garden. He was going to secure the line inside the fence where we were then standing. Thus, if I wanted to make contact with him, all I had to do was to reach over the fence and give the line a sharp tug. Needless to say, we enjoyed our tea and cakes that night, and there was always a good cuppa waiting for us whenever we were on perimeter patrol again.

I was woken up early one morning by someone opening the door of our hut. Whoever it was then shouted out, 'Anyone here want a paper?' I knew the voice, it was my young brother Ken. By the time I had focused my eyes, there he stood in the doorway with an armful of newspapers.

Close to the camp was a newspaper shop which I knew well, known as The Golf House, from the time when this whole area had been in fact a public golf course. Ken had obviously been told where I was stationed, had gone into the shop and offered his services as a newsboy to sell newspapers in the camp. I was delighted to see him, and admired his audacity in gaining access to the camp by this means. Thereafter, he called on me early on many occasions, but unbeknown to me, I would not be staying at this particular location much longer.

I was beginning to thoroughly enjoy my new lifestyle, but it was not long before things began to change. While cleaning my kit one morning, I heard a clamour of Scottish voices. Looking up, I noticed that an army truck had arrived at the camp gate and was being checked by the guard. The vehicle then came in and stopped at the parking area, where about twenty Scots in kilts got off. It was the London Scottish Regiment, and what they were doing in our area, I did not know.

They were then ordered on parade, and marched to the front of the club house. I could not imagine Scots transferring to a Welsh regiment, but could not think of any reason for them being here I then walked round to the front of the building myself and, to my surprise, saw the newcomers being marched over to the gun emplacements.

That evening, the Jocks left us and numerous speculative rumours circulated. The favourite was that we were going overseas, and the Jocks were going to take over our gun site. Trust the Jocks, we thought: we do all the work and get the gun site prepared, and they just walk in to a purpose-built location!

The rumours continued, but the most that the speculation produced was one positive statement from Sergeant Williams, the one man who probably knew the truth of the matter. He told us that we definitely would be going to a firing camp in Wales in the near future and, as for the London Scottish, they would be looking after our gun site while we were away. That was as far as he was prepared to go. Then, almost as if he was enjoying the situation, he ended by telling us that we were now facing a very well thought out training schedule, and we would not be spending so much time in the canteen once it started.

The first part of this so-called training programme started the following morning. After breakfast we were led to the gun pits. There we were given a most interesting lecture on the fusing of the anti-aircraft shells. Most of us, I am sure, had stopped to think just how it was that soldiers managed to work out the mathematics of the problem facing them. Just consider it for a moment. Having first of all sighted the plane, decide where it will be when the gun is fired, calculate the height of the plane, the wind speed and barometric pressure. Then, using those figures, work out the correct bearing and angle of the guns, and fuse the ammunition so that the shell explodes and destroys the plane.

This mass of information was fed into various instruments at the Command Post, from where the orders to set the fuses and fire the guns were given.

We listened attentively, taking in as much as we could absorb. From the way it was explained, however, one could be excused for thinking that there was no way one could miss hitting an enemy plane. To a man, we knew that this could not be so, and said so to the instructor. He smiled, then stood for a minute thinking. Then, having sorted out his answer in his mind, he said, 'If everything is done immediately, the information put in immediately, and the command from the Command Post is acted upon immediately, the plane should be hit. The margin of error comes when there is the slightest delay in acting upon the instructions, for the plane will be travelling at a very fast speed, and every second is a hundred feet towards an error.'

This was a most interesting lecture, but the more the instructor spoke, the more convinced we were that he was speaking 'from the book' and not from experience. We certainly needed experience, and the projected firing camp in Wales could not come fast enough for all of us.

There was a lot of talk in the canteen that night. Quite a few of those present had been to a firing camp earlier in their service in the Territorial Army. They all agreed with our instructor's last statement. Yes, the instruments could work out everything for you, but while this was going on the plane was also going on, and on, and on, getting further or nearer. Whatever the delay, it had to be in feet and perhaps hundreds of feet. A direct hit would be in the order of a hundred feet. On this point we were agreed.

We put our observations to our instructor the following morning. He agreed that one hundred feet would be a direct hit. He then went on to tell us how a good Command Post officer could correct the firing from his first shot, something that came only from experience. He was pleased to hear that we had taken in everything he had said, and also that we were discussing his talk amongst ourselves.

His last words, however, were that we also would learn more from experience than just talking about it. Furthermore, we would shortly be having that experience. I felt that we had given the instructor quite a lot to think about. We parted the best of friends, and agreed that there was a lot of good common sense in what he had said.

Sergeant Williams sent for me the next day. He told me that I had been put forward for an explosives course at Bishop Stortford. Transport had been arranged, and I would be leaving camp at noon. He then gave me a piece of paper introducing me to a Captain in the Royal Engineers at Bishop Stortford, and bearing his address. At noon I left Norbury, and travelled to the address given. It was a large country house in some woods at the edge of Bishop Stortford. The driver told me that he would come and pick me up in two days' time, as directed.

I had been told to take my small kit with me, and on arrival I was met by a Royal Engineers Sergeant who took me to a room containing beds. He directed me to one, and told me that was where I would sleep for the next two nights. He then showed me to the mess room and canteen. I felt like a perfect stranger who had met friends, and the Sergeant seemed the perfect host. Breakfast would be at 8am, after which I would be told where to go for the talk. I then made my way to the mess room and met four lads from other regiments who had joined the course that day, and had an enjoyable tea together. Bread, jam and cakes, with plenty of tea.

The following morning, after breakfast, those on the course were directed to a beautifully panelled room. There were eight of us in this class, all from the Royal Artillery. We were directed to take our place in some comfortable armchairs by the Royal Engineer Captain in charge. He told us that we would incur his wrath if any of us were to fall asleep. The object of the course, he said, was to instill in our minds the danger of explosives, with particular attention being paid to unexploded shells and bombs. He did not want us to think that he was going to make bomb disposal men out of us; he just wanted to make sure that everyone who passed through his hands knew enough about the dangers involved to send for the experts.

The captain went on to explain that unexploded shells are rarely dangerous, so he would not go into that one. If you come across an unexploded shell, he told us, the best thing to do is to blow it up, having first taken it somewhere safe for that purpose.

He also asked us to always remember to 'Send for the experts, it's no trouble to them, and they know what they're doing.' He continued by warning us to make no mistake about the fact that unexploded bombs are dangerous, and to regard every one as being about to go off.

'You will have heard about the ways we, the Royal Engineers, deal with bombs, and maybe you have watched demonstrations on the subject. Bombs are made to explode when they land, to kill people and damage property. It is just the evil in man that tampers with them and booby-traps from them when made, thus bringing a fresh danger into this side of the war.

'There is a fuse-cum-detonator in the side of bombs. It was originally put there to enable the military to disarm them if they did not explode on impact. That, however, was too easy. The powers-that-be decided there was something else they could do, and they booby-trapped their bombs in advance. Some were not even meant to explode on impact, but to kill a few clever soldiers as well.

'The first efforts at disarming bombs were simple. With a two pronged key, the soldiers just had to unscrew and remove the fuse. No problem. Then they wired the fuse to another small detonator under the fuse. The Sapper would then unscrew the fuse and carefully lift it out in the approved manner. 'Bang'. No more Sapper.

'Since then there have been many other very dangerous changes made, until the only probable safe method of disarming a bomb was by what we in the Royal Engineers call the Chinese Laundry method - drilling two holes in the bomb and steaming the charge out. You, gentlemen, have been sent here to learn about bombs, and the most important thing you have learned, which you must take away with you, is to send for the experts. Don't fiddle with bombs: they are dangerous, they are made to go off - explode and kill.'

I left Bishop Stortford feeling that I had learned a lot, and with great respect for the Royal Engineers.

Dispatch Rider Wanted

Shortly after leaving school, I had taken up cycle racing. I had good balance and road sense, therefore the job I wanted in the army was as a dispatch rider.

I had never ridden a motorcycle, and must have had a lot of cheek. Yet I had driven my father's car in car parks and out of the way places, and was sure that I could ride and control a motorcycle. So I spent a lot of time near the Battery Office, where the dispatch riders congregated and parked their machines. I studied the controls and watched the riders come and go very intently. Soon I became very friendly with one of them, Gunner Derek Downes-Powell. I could not imagine that riding a motorcycle would be very difficult. In fact, given the chance, I felt quite satisfied in my mind that I could ride one. I continued watching the dispatch riders, and studied their activities on every possible occasion.

Then the great day came. A notice appeared on the Battery notice board. 'Dispatch Rider Wanted - Apply to the Battery Clerk.' I marched straight into Battery Office and asked for the job.

Sergeant Williams immediately said to me, 'Can you ride a motorcycle?'

'Of course I can,' I lied politely. There was then some discussion between the Sergeant and an officer who had come into the office behind me, a conversation I could not hear. The Sergeant then took a chequebook from a drawer and wrote out a cheque which he asked the officer to sign. Having signed it, the officer gave it to me. It was for £30.

'Go to Pride & Clarke's in Brixton and get yourself a motorcycle,' he said. I looked at the cheque and then at the officer. No doubt he read my thoughts. 'It's all right,' he said, 'they're all at the same price.'

The Sergeant then said, 'Get hold of Downes-Powell, he'll take you there.'

I saluted and left the office, praising my good fortune, but at the same time wondering just what I had let myself in for. I was not a little excited and loitered in the vicinity of Battery Office, waiting impatiently for the return of Downes-Powell. He finally returned to camp at 2.30pm and I explained to him what had taken place earlier in Battery Office. He was not in the slightest bit surprised, and didn't even bother to dismount. 'Hop on the back,' he said, so I climbed on to the pillion seat behind him and we drove off.

On our way to Brixton, I watched Downe-Powell's every move with the controls. I was so engrossed with my inspection that the next thing I knew, we were easing to a halt in a yard off Stockwell Road, Brixton, leading to an area where there was a row of motorcycles. A man who appeared to be in charge came over to us. He knew exactly what we wanted. 'Got your cheque?' he asked, smiling. I handed it over. He examined it fairly closely then, turning to Downes-Powell, said, 'You've been here before, haven't you?' Derek replied that he had, and the man replied, 'Help yourself', indicating the row of motorcycles.

I walked along the line of motorcycles which to my young eyes were beautiful - just nineteen years old and attempting to look knowledgeable! I had no idea what I was supposed to look for, and dared not ask my colleague for an opinion. Stopping in front of an A.J.S. Silver Streak, I was very conscious of being closely watched by the salesman. I had to say something. 'Let's have a look at that one,' I said, and indicated the A.J.S. The salesman brought the machine out, and put it on its stand.

I walked round this quite impressive motor cycle, attempting to look knowledgeable. 'Start it up,' I said. This was done. 'Sounds all right,' I said, 'but just take it up the alleyway, it looks as if it's had a knock and is slightly out of track.' The man shook his head, muttered something under his breath and gave me a very odd look, but nevertheless did as I asked. He drove the machine up the alleyway, turned and came back to me. 'Great,' I said. 'Sorry about that, don't switch off, I'll take it.'

The salesman got off the machine, and I got on. He said nothing but I could see out of the corner of my eye that he was watching me very closely. I kept asking myself whether I was going to make it and going through the actions of what I had to do next. There was no going back now, so I drew in the clutch and kicked up the foot gear change into first gear. All right so far. I did so much want to look in the salesman's direction and bid him a parting farewell, but had enough trouble keeping control of the bike.

I built up the engine revolutions slightly as I let out the clutch slowly. Then I took off with a bit of a leap, and thankfully, I managed to control the machine. I was glad that I had not turned my head to look at the salesman. At the end of the alleyway, I turned left into Stockwell Road, and headed towards the centre of Brixton, with the large Bon Marché store on my right hand side. The traffic lights at the junction were red. I therefore slowed down until they went green, then turned right.

I made my way through Brixton and up Brixton Hill. Downes-Powell by this time was frantic. I had not changed gear, and was for the time being happy that the machine was moving steadily in the direction that I wanted to travel. My colleague, however, was shouting at me, but I was far too busy with the task in hand to pay any attention to him.

By the time we arrived at Streatham Tate Library, having travelled some three or four miles still in first gear, I knew something had to be done. Downes-Powell was not at all happy. He was calling me every type of idiot he could put his tongue to. He was going to report me. I was going to land up in the Guard Room. In his rage, he then tried to outline to me the many and various charges I had laid myself open to. I waited patiently until he had finished his tirade of abuse, then calmly told him that I disagreed. This made matters even worse and he became quite uncontrollable in his rage and frustration.

When Downes-Powell finally calmed down, I pointed out to him that if he was going to do anything, he should have done it at Stockwell Road. Being the expert motorcyclist that he was supposed to be, he should have known at the outset that I could not ride a motorcycle. I also pointed out that the Commanding Officer was not going to be very happy with the Orderly Officer and Battery Clerk who had permitted all this to happen.

I then quietly suggested that if we spent a few minutes in the back streets, where we were then stationary, and I took a few lessons from him there and then, I would be able to ride back into camp and nobody would be any the wiser. Needless to say, while I was saying all this, I was inwardly praying that he would do as I asked.

Reluctantly, very reluctantly, he agreed to my suggestion, but he was clearly unhappy about the whole matter he just waved farewell and rode off back to camp. The result, however, was that I did ride back into camp that day in an apparently acceptable manner.

Nobody discovered my secret, and I continued to ride motorcycles in many countries throughout the war without mishap. I have to admit, however, that some of the most hair-raising experiences I ever had on a motorcycle were while riding as a dispatch rider or on other business in London during the early days of the blackout.

There were many unusual happenings in those days. Few of us had any first-hand knowledge of war, or of army life. Most of us, in fact, were convinced in our ignorance that the war would be over in six months or less. We were all so firmly convinced that the Germans were no match for us. Furthermore, we were also convinced that our sojourn in the army was just another piece of drudgery that we would have to turn into something of a holiday until we went back to our civilian jobs. We had much to learn

I was happy in my knowledge of London and its environs, and found it most useful. My journeys were generally to the same areas: over to Lea Green where 48th Brigade offices were situated; to Kidbrook, where the Royal Army Ordnance Corps had a massive store; to Regimental Headquarters in the Wickham Court Hotel in West Wickham, Kent; and also to 302 Battery Headquarters. These lucky people were situated in the beautiful house and grounds that I was told had belonged to a famous writer, at the edge of Hayes Common, only a mile from the Hayes Common gun site of 303 Battery, where I made very regular calls.

This was a section of 303 Battery where troops manned four 3-inch naval anti-aircraft guns. The section had been quarantined because many of the troops stationed there had broken out in a rash similar to measles. Furthermore, some of them had been taken into hospital suffering from German measles. The medical officer was in quite a quandary about it, and rather than take chances, he had placed the troops in quarantine until such time as his research came up with an answer. The troops, however, blamed the food, and maybe they were right. They were convinced that whatever was being cooked in those dixies, which were cleaned out after every meal, must hold the key to the whole matter. Perhaps they were not cleaned as they should have been, despite the fact that they had passed inspection. Also, none of the troops were used to the type of food being served.

No one was allowed either in or out of the Hayes Common Camp perimeter. Thus, when I called at the camp, I would place my dispatches in a postbox at the side of the guardroom, and take out whatever had to go back to Battery Headquarters. These calls were generally no more than routine, and more often than not I would not even get off my motorcycle to deliver and collect.

On one particular occasion, however, Sergeant Owen, the Troop Commander, wanted to speak to me. The sentry called out the Guard Commander, who in turn brought Sergeant Owen to where I was waiting by the guardroom. The Sergeant was a strict disciplinarian who would not tolerate inefficiency or disobedience of any kind. Faced with the quarantine, Gunner Jones, B had left the camp and was absent without leave.

I was directed to inform Battery Sergeant Major Giles on my return; he would forward a covering report immediately his Hayes enquiries were completed. I returned to Norbury and passed on this information to Major Giles. He was absolutely furious, and ranted and raved about the calibre of men who, in his words, dared to call themselves soldiers just because there was a war on. I was pleased to leave his presence. Quite apart from his personal feelings, this incident certainly did cause quite a stir.

The absent Gunner, Barry Jones, was an accountant in peacetime, and that was all we really knew of his background. He was generally known as something of a practical joker, and one who was never lost for an answer. Unfortunately for him, he was also known to be a rebel against some of the petty disciplines meted out by his superiors, Sergeant Owen being one. The true story, however, unfolded later that day when Gunner Jones, B returned to camp of his own free will.

Earlier that morning, Jones had arrived on parade, turned out in a manner which probably offended King's Regulations, and certainly offended Sergeant Owen. His forage cap was not on straight, his jacket was not properly fastened, and his boots were dirty. As a result, he was placed on fatigues. That morning, all normal fatigue duties had already been allocated. He was therefore handed a long metal spike of the type used by park-keepers, and told to go round the camp and pick up litter.

Barry Jones saluted, turned and left the Sergeant's office, bearing the spike. Sergeant Owen was somewhat dumbfounded. Jones did not have to salute him, for he was not a commissioned officer. At the same time, he did not make an issue of it, knowing Jones as he did. Jones did his round of the camp, and on finding no more scraps to pick up, returned to the Sergeant's office to report the situation. Like a good soldier, he stood smartly to attention, again saluted, and reported the fact that he could find no more litter.

The Sergeant said nothing. He got up, stood at the entrance of his office, pointed to a number of leaves on the ground outside and barked, 'What about that lot? Now get on with it and don't trouble me again. I've got enough to do just now!' He turned and strode back into his office. Gunner Jones was quite content to get on with the job in hand, for in truth, he had little else to do, since everyone was confined to camp. On the other hand, he was silently enjoying himself, playing a game of cat and mouse with the Sergeant, even in the full knowledge that he could never win the game.

To Gunner Jones this was partly a bit of fun, but he was undoubtedly also driven by the fact that he was inwardly rebelling against performing these unnecessary tasks that the confinement demanded.

He got on with his task until midday, then once more returned to the Sergeant's office. 'Sarge, I've picked up all of the rubbish,' he said, flourishing his spike, now filled with leaves and pieces of paper. The Sergeant did not get up. Glowering at Jones, he said, 'Now get out of here, and get on with your job.' Then looking down at his work, or whatever he had in front of him on his desk, he waved Jones out of his office.

That superior wave may have disposed of lesser men, but not Gunner Jones. Although inwardly chuckling because he now felt he was on a winning streak, he hung his head and in a plaintive voice said, 'But where shall I look now? I can't find any more, Sarge.'

The Sergeant stood up and thumped his desk - an army-issue table folded flat, and bellowed, 'Get out! Get out of my sight!' Jones now knew that he was winning and, still with an air of injured innocence, enquired, 'But where shall I look now, Sarge?' The Sergeant, in a somewhat tired manner, looked up and said, 'Anywhere, just get out of here, out of my sight.' Jones was happy now; in his mind he had won the battle of wits. He saluted smartly, turned, and with an inward chuckle left the Sergeant.

Now it was not difficult to leave the camp area unnoticed. The perimeter fence in those days consisted of two strands of barbed wire, and only part of this was in sight of the guardroom or the sentry on duty. Gunner Jones just walked round the perimeter wire picking up leaves and odd pieces of rubbish, until he saw that the coast was clear. He then calmly walked down the road towards Bromley, and hid his spike in the bushes. In Bromley, he entered the first public house he saw and consumed a couple of pints of beer, during which time he no doubt chuckled some more.

After his refreshment, and no doubt because closing time demanded it, he left the public house and slowly sauntered back to camp. On the way, he recovered his spike and filled it to the limit. Satisfied that he had completed his task to the best of his ability, he was not at all disturbed when he was seized by the Guard Commander and placed in the guardroom. The Sergeant was sent for, and Jones was later marched in to the Troop Sergeant's presence.

'What have you to say for yourself?' yelled the Sergeant.

'I've filled the spike, Sarge,' replied Jones, indicating the spike that was now propped up in the corner of the guardroom.

'Who told you to leave camp?' bellowed the Sergeant.

'You did, Sarge,' replied Jones. 'I told you I'd cleaned up the camp and asked you where to go next. You told me to go anywhere. I went down the road outside the camp until the spikes were filled up, then came back to camp immediately. What's the trouble Sarge?'

I will not repeat the Sergeant's reply or tell you what action he took in relation to this rather unusual incident. I can only say that the result was that Gunner Jones became quite a good soldier.

There is little doubt that Gunner Barry Jones took to heart the words of rage vented on him by Sergeant Owen that day. He was also most fortunate in the fact that the Quarantine Order had been rescinded that morning. Had it not been, there would have been real trouble in store for this soldier. I can say, however, that although the story circulated around the regiment like wildfire, in one form or another, there were no further incidents of a similar nature.

I was thoroughly enjoying my new role as a dispatch rider. My machine behaved perfectly but, considering the novelty of my new-found ability to ride a motorcycle, I might have been a little over-confident. As if to prove this point, I was returning from 48th Brigade Headquarters at Lee Green on one dull afternoon in November when I was brought rather abruptly to my senses. It was raining very slightly, and I was cursing the probability of getting wet through in my leather jerkin before arriving back at camp.

I was travelling in Brownhill Road towards Catford at about twenty-five miles an hour. As I approached the 'T' junction with Rushey Green, I changed gear and slowed down, intending to turn left at the junction. The road to my right was clear and on the other side of the road, a tram car was approaching.

But as I turned left at the junction, the motorcycle slid from under me. Luckily, I managed to free myself from the machine, then heard the *ping ping ping* as the tram driver hit his alarm bell. There was a loud crack as the driver lowered the ancient but very efficient cow-catcher under the front of the tram. This was followed by a crunching sound as he released grit and applied his brakes. As for my beloved motorcycle, it slid neatly under the tram, scooped up in the cow-catcher. This all happened in a matter of seconds, and I was quite taken aback by the speed of it all. I got to my feet and went over to the tram. The very red-faced and somewhat aged tram driver climbed down from his cab, muttering something about 'Bloody young soldiers who should be in France.'

I tried to extract my machine from under the front of the tram, but it was stuck fast. By now, the driver was getting very impatient, and demanding to see my insurance certificate. I told him that I was an army dispatch rider on duty, and that the motorcycle belonged to the army. His answer to this was to scratch his head and say, 'Bloody funny army bike, all chrome-plated!'

At that point, the driver of a motor car that had stopped nearby and was sympathetic towards me came forward and joined me. He quietened the tram driver, and assisted us to get the motorcycle free. Needless to say, there was no damage to the tram, or for that matter to the very useful if somewhat ancient cow-catcher. There were, however, some nasty looking scrapes on the mudguards of my motorcycle. Apart from that, it seemed to be in good order. Happily, the tram driver did not want my particulars; I had no intention of reporting the matter and becoming involved in the aggravation that an enquiry would entail. I therefore did not take his details either.

We parted company with his words still ringing in my ears: 'Take care in future, young soldier, you may not be so lucky next time.' On my way back to camp, I purchased a tin of Bluebell metal polish and obtained some rag. As it was still raining, I stopped under Hermitage Bridge in Norbury and cleaned up the scrape marks as best as I could. I did not want the Orderly Officer, or anyone else for that matter, questioning me, although, it must have been fairly obvious what had happened.

Right now, when I look back on those years, I find it difficult to suppress a chuckle. Being a dispatch rider was a somewhat hazardous task, not unglamorous, and it kept me away from guard duties and fatigues. I had never seen a crash helmet except in films, and as far as I was concerned, they had not been issued. There was no such thing as an army issue raincoat for motorcyclists;

the army leather jerkin was the order of the day. Then there was the most important article of all, boots motorcyclist dispatch riders for the use of. Not available.

We badgered the Quartermaster for these boots despite him telling us so firmly that they were not available. Once, during his absence, I looked these items up in one of his issue books in his store. This was the Quartermaster's handbook, the mythical G1098 that set out the items of clothing and equipment to which we were entitled. Oh yes, both the boots, motorcycle dispatch riders for the use of, and raincoats, motorcyclists were there.

While I was browsing through his 'Bible' the Quartermaster came into the store. 'What the hell are you doing here with that book?' he said. I told him that I had been speaking to a dispatch rider at 48th Brigade Headquarters, and he had said that both the boots and the raincoats were available. To my complete surprise, the Quartermaster just sat down at his desk and went into quite a long story of the amount of work he had done to get us these items. By the time I left, I had no doubt that he had already made a lot of effort to get us properly equipped.

From other sources, we soon learned that our Quartermaster had worked extremely hard to get our correct equipment issued. The trouble in those early days of the war was that there were so many volunteers for the services to be equipped; so many that what had been in store was mostly needed for the troops in France. Certainly he sympathised with us; our plight had been amply demonstrated to him on a number of occasions when we returned to camp soaked to the skin, having been obliged to travel in the pouring rain without proper protection.

In truth we felt fortunate to have a Quartermaster with such feelings. Our regular soakings were the last straw to him. He summoned us to his presence one morning, and we wondered just what 'Q' wanted us for. He handed each dispatch rider an official note addressed to Montague Burton, the tailors in Brixton Road, London. All he said was, 'Don't open it, just take it there.'

Once out of Quartermaster's store, we all looked at the notes: we each had an order for one raincoat. We were surprised and intended to tell 'Q' so when we returned to camp. The note may have been one surprise, but once inside Burton's, our surprise was even greater. There were beautiful gabardine raincoats with oilskin between the lining and the outer covering. Undoubtedly officer issue, but extremely comfortable and ideal for our purpose.

About this time (the same period as the quarantine order at Hayes Common gun site), members of our Battery from other sites were taken ill. They were immediately taken to the Royal Herbert Military Hospital on the outskirts of the garrison town of Woolwich. It was to this hospital that I rode with their first mail. Proud as Punch, and extremely smart in my new Montague Burton raincoat, I stopped outside the hospital. The all-important letters were secured by an elastic band in my inside raincoat pocket.

I pulled the motorcycle up on to its stand and walked towards the sentry. I had been warned that this was a military hospital, and I might not be allowed inside but would have to deliver the letters to the guardroom. The sentry, to my surprise, snapped sharply to attention and threw up a smart salute. I thought perhaps that he knew me and was taking the mickey out of my attire. I said nothing, returned his greeting in a cross between a salute and a wave, and walked past him. I could see the Sergeant of the guard at the guardroom door and believed that he was possibly expecting me. He likewise saluted, and I knew that something had to be done. I returned the salute to the best of my ability, but in a similar fashion and asked him to direct me to Ward 6. His directions were crisps and accurate. I nodded, and continued in the direction indicated.

At the entrance of the second floor ward, a nurse came out of the side room to enquire what I wanted. I produced my letters and said I would like to see the men of my unit. (I was now full of my new-found confidence, born undoubtedly from the near royal greeting I'd received from the sentry and the guard commander.) To my surprise, the nurse just laughed, and her next remark confirmed to me that she was no fool. 'I don't know how you got this far,' she said. 'Only M.Os [Medical Officers] and staff are allowed here. This is a quarantine area, you know.' I put on my best front of complete ignorance and apology, handed her the letters and asked if she could see if there was anything any of the lads wanted, or any message that I could take from them. The nurse agreed and went about her work. On her return, I thanked her and indicated that I might return the following day if there were further letters to be delivered. To this her reply was, 'You might not be so lucky next time, so be sure that you leave everything you have with the guard commander.' She then turned and walked away down the ward.

My return to the Battery Office on the Westminster Bank Sports Ground was greeted with some surprise when I mentioned what had happened. John Williams, the Battery clerk, did not think that it was a very clever thing to have done. He then went on to detail the many and various forms of punishment that I could have been liable to had I been caught by an officious person. I accepted his criticism and words of advice, but it had been something of a challenge and I had to admit that I had enjoyed the experience.

The following day, amongst the various items to be taken around to my usual stopping places, was a package of letters for Ward 6 at the Royal Herbert Hospital. This time I would do strictly as directed and hand them over to the Guard Commander.

Wise men have been known to say on many occasions that the best laid plans of mice and men go astray at times. I did not know it when I decided on my course of action following that talk with Sergeant Williams, but my honourable intentions were not to be.

Arriving outside the Royal Herbert Hospital once again, I pulled the motorcycle up on its stand as before. Then as I turned towards the sentry, he threw me up a salute that would have delighted King George V himself. At the same time, he bellowed at the top of his voice, 'All present and correct, Saaaah.' Without thinking, or perhaps inspired by the impressive salute, I waved a form of salute towards the guard and walked over to the guardroom. The Sergeant clattered to the guardroom door immediately he heard the sentry's loud greeting. He likewise acknowledged me in a most impressive manner. This was just too much. I did not have it in me to inform him that he was mistaken, and that I was not an officer. I saluted him in passing, and once again made my way to Ward 6.

The nurse who greeted me on this occasion was older than the one I had met on the previous day, probably in her thirties. I handed her the letters and asked if there were any messages to take back.

There was then a sudden and most distinct change in her attitude. 'Ah yes,' she said, 'you came yesterday.'

'That's right,' I replied.

'Only officers and staff are allowed here,' she said. 'You are neither an officer or a member of our staff. I will deliver the letters now, and on my return I shall telephone the Guard Commander. If you are still within the precincts of this hospital, you will be arrested, and I would not like to think what will happen to you then.' She turned and marched off into the ward.

There was no mistaking the point, I had to get out, and quickly. I have no idea whether or not the nurse did telephone the guardroom. I do know, however, that I did leave the hospital in a great hurry, and never wore my Montague Burton raincoat on subsequent visits to the Royal Herbert Hospital. The traditional army leather jerkin, my obvious Gunners uniform, was always clearly visible when I called on future occasions.

A Limber Gunner

On my return to Norbury, I found that a lot had happened that day. Various troops of the regiment were going to places around London setting up gun sites for future use. Furthermore, the feeling that I got when delivering dispatches was that I was just another labourer. There seemed to be no future in being a dispatch rider, although there was variety in the work. At least I had learned to ride a motorcycle, and that was a pleasure itself.

The move that really interested me was that 303 Battery now had a large gun site on the top of the Shirley Hills, near the old militia camp that had been built the previous year. This was above Shirley Park Golf Course, and was now occupied by many of the Battery personnel. I decided to return to the gun crews and let this fact be known. There were many who wanted my job as a dispatch rider, so this caused no concern. I decided to become a Limber Gunner

To the uninitiated, a Limber Gunner is something of a grease monkey-cum-mechanic, generally seen in the vicinity of the guns, dressed in overalls and carrying an oilcan, a piece of rag and a spanner. He is very rarely seen on parades, fatigues or guard duty. Proud of the internal and external condition and operation of the guns under his care, he looks out for any defects and is able to carry out exchanges of faulty and worn parts.

Apart from the obvious advantages of being able to avoid the tiresome number of extra duties, I took this job in order to enlarge my very deep interest in but limited knowledge of artillery pieces. In my spare time since joining the regiment, I had studied the handbooks of the 3-inch and 3.7-inch anti aircraft guns to the extent that I knew almost every nut and bolt by the correct (and often peculiar) name. Interested parties had even come to me for advice on how to operate what I was beginning to look upon as 'my' gun, and frankly I was proud of how much information I had managed to take in.

This was soon common knowledge in the Battery, and when I was approached by the Orderly Officer on the gun site and asked to take on the job of Limber Gunner, I was quite shocked. He greeted me like a long-lost friend, welcoming me to the job in a way that was a little embarrassing.

You may be wondering why I sought out the job of grease monkey. The answer is simple. There had been times when officers and Sergeants of the Royal Army Ordnance Corps had come to the camp to either set up or align the guns at Norbury. They were always highly respected, and knew their jobs so well. I wanted to learn that trade. I felt in my heart that if they could do it, with a little effort why could I not learn myself? Thereafter, I was always on the gun site, and made a very good job of the work. It was dirty work, of course, but the results were always most satisfying. I learned the function of the breech mechanism and was soon able to strip it down and reassemble it blindfold. I also gave talks on the operation of the gun to the gun crews.

My new lifestyle as a Limber Gunner had other good points, apart from the fact that we were not called upon for guard duties and general fatigues. Here at the Shirley Battery headquarters, the Limber Gunners seemed to have far more opportunity to visit Croydon and even London.

My knowledge of London was well known, and I was often invited to accompany members of the Battery there for some form of minor celebration. One such invitation came my way when one of our number, Albert Jones, decided to celebrate his second wedding anniversary. This was to take place at a public house called The Bedford Head in Maiden Lane, Covent Garden. We caught a bus from Shirley to East Croydon railway station, and then a train to Victoria Station in London.

At The Bedford Head, a good time was had by all. Bert Jones' wife was waiting for us, and we ate and drank well. We left the public house in good time to be able to return to camp by our 10pm deadline, and headed for Victoria Station.

Bert and I decided to walk to Victoria Station from the Covent Garden area, while the remainder of the company decided to go by various forms of public transport. On arrival at the station, there was an almost empty train, the fast one to East Croydon, waiting for us. We boarded and had a small carriage to ourselves. We were soon fast asleep, probably thanks to the fact that we had drunk a little more than usual.

We were somewhat rudely woken from our reverie by a noise that suggested we were being attacked. The train was moving very slowly and we found to our surprise that we were travelling through one of those peculiar train-washing sheds. Water was being sprayed over the train and a series of rotating brushes were cleaning down the side of the carriages. The *boom boom boom* of these brushes on the side of the train sounded to us almost like gunfire. Bert Jones looked over to me, and said, 'Where the hell are we, John?' I looked at my watch: we had been on the train for over four hours. I told him that I thought we had arrived at Brighton.

Within a few minutes, the brushing on the side of the carriages stopped. The train pulled out of the shed, stopped on a siding and all went quiet. About an hour after that, the train started up and pulled in to the platform of Brighton Station. It was a quarter to four in the morning, and all Bert could say was that we would now land up in the Guardroom. I saw a lone porter sweeping up the platform, and went over to him. 'Where the hell did you come from?' he asked. I told him that we had caught the train from Victoria Station at about nine o'clock the previous night and were supposed to get out at East Croydon. He began to laugh.

I was joined by Bert, who had come out of the carriage because of the laughter. 'What now?' he asked.

The porter stifled his laughter and said, 'The best thing you can do is to come to my room and have a cup of tea. This train will be leaving in a half hour, and it'll stop at East Croydon.' We joined our porter in his room, and had a very welcome cup of tea. After that, he said the best thing we should do was to get back on to the train before someone started asking silly questions as to why we were there at all. We thanked our porter friend, said our goodbyes and made for the train.

We arrived at East Croydon at half past six that morning. There were other people on the train, and we got amongst them to surrender our tickets. Fortunately, the ticket collector was half asleep, and we left the station hastily, then made our way back to camp at Shirley in quick time. There, Lady Luck was with us: we had not been missed and, after volunteering to assist the cooks, we were soon consuming a very healthy breakfast of bacon, eggs and tomatoes with a mug of tea from the cook's dixie.

When certain members of the regiment moved to various gun sites around London, this aroused a glut of rumours that we were on the move - reinforced to some extent by the fact that we received an intake of young men from Liverpool, who were referred to as 'immatures'. They were in fact young men from a regiment that had been dispatched to France, but in view of their ages (under nineteen), they had been posted to the London Welsh. This was only to make up for those of our own regiment who had likewise been sent to join another regiment prior to going to France or elsewhere.

It was soon Christmas and the rumour-mongers had decided that we were definitely on the move. Aberporth was the reputed destination, and the Welshmen amongst us who came from that area were convinced that they would be home for the New Year. This was something I felt should happen. It was logical, but I was not convinced that the army always did logical things. In fact, during my extremely short service, there seemed to be many illogical decisions made within the regiment.

But that, of course, was only my opinion at the time.

Aberporth Firing Camp

The Welsh voices had done us proud over the Christmas festivities, and there had been promises of a very special New Year's Eve Party. In the late afternoon of New Year's Eve, however, a large number of Royal Army Service Corps vehicles arrived on the gun site and camp, suggesting that our move was imminent. Those who professed to know put forward various suggested locations, from France to places around London. But there was still a fairly strong contingent which favoured Aberporth.

Late in the afternoon, we were put on these lorries, complete with kit. So much for the promised New Year's Eve party! We left Shirley at six o'clock and were driven to Paddington Railway Station in London. There we de-bussed and lined up on one of the platforms. Later that night we were loaded on to an empty train. Those of us who knew London were convinced that it was Wales for us, as Paddington trains were all for the west country and Wales. Aberporth had to be our next location.

The journey was not all that comfortable, although we dozed through the night, finally stopping at Newcastle Emlyn at daybreak. There, many lorries were waiting for us, civilian lorries with civilian drivers. We were bundled into these and driven off. The type of driving, however, was something very new to me, and very frightening indeed. This area was very hilly, far more than any other area I had previously been to, and the lorries were heavily laden, with not even the smallest space wasted. They would literally groan their way up the hills then, once over the crest, the driver would disengage the gears and coast down the other side at a terrifying rate of knots - to save petrol, I was told! However, we made it and luckily there were no mishaps but I was far from being the only one who was scared stiff during some of those descents

The firing camp was very interesting, though there were times when I really began to wonder whether we would ever have a chance of hitting an enemy plane. Put yourself in my position in those days: I was a total stranger to the concepts we had to consider, and the instruments involved. There was the Predictor, the Heightfinder and the Rangefinder. Then I had to take into consideration the windspeed, the temperature, the barometric pressure at mean sea level, and umpteen other unusual points. After all that, there was the small matter of putting the information into instruments that we had never previously used. Our instructors were for the most part regular soldiers, probably promoted years in advance of the norm. We were willing and anxious to learn, but our confusion had to be experienced to be appreciated.

I was pleased to find that our first day on the actual range was a fine one. A small aircraft appeared from our left, way out to sea, drawing behind it what looked like a long piece of cloth. This, we were told, was the sleeve. The object of the exercise was to hit the Sleeve. Don't lay on, aim at the plane, we were told. This direction was given to the layers on each gun, the men with the bearing and angle dials, and I have to admit that the temptation was always to aim directly at the plane.

Our first few shots went very wide, and my personal worry was for the pilot, who must have had a lot of guts. It made me wonder whether the Royal Air Force also had fatigues for pilots, and if perhaps this was how their Sergeant Majors got their own back on unruly pilots. Some shells exploded behind the sleeve, others exploded between the sleeve and the plane. Afterwards we were gathered together for a pep talk by the I.G. - Instructor of Gunnery - and later returned to the range for further practice.

Returning to the gun site, we repeated the procedure and soon seemed to be getting our shells nearer to the target. Then, for reasons that I shall never understand, a shell exploded immediately under the towing plane

There was an absolute outburst from the Command Post, with loud hoarse orders of 'Cease firing!' The plane released the sleeve far out to sea and flew straight at us, missing the guns by what seemed like inches before turning and disappearing over the horizon. Needless to say, everyone, including our officers, was subjected to some pretty intense lectures after this incident.

I am glad to say that after some further concentrated practice, we managed to pass out under the eagle eyes of the Gunnery Instructors. It was, of course, wartime; I doubt very much whether we would have passed out during peacetime.

My first Sunday at Aberporth was memorable for a number of reasons. We had our church parade in the morning and after that, with the exception of those on duty, we were allowed out of camp. I had never been to Wales before, and knew little about Welsh customs and ways. Before joining the army, I could count the number of pints I had consumed on one hand with ease.

Since joining the London Welsh, however, with the canteen the only place for recreation and relaxation, I had learned to appreciate a good pint of beer. I did try ginger ale on one occasion to quench my thirst, but as I picked up the glass, the canteen went silent, with everyone staring at me. I changed my canteen drinking habits after that.

I had one good friend in the Battery, Tom Goodfellow, who was born in nearby Cardigan. One day I got into conversation with him about the locality. As the evening drew on I asked him if he fancied going into Aberporth town for a drink. I was in for a culture shock.

'If you live in a town in Wales, you can't drink there on a Sunday,' Tom told me. 'If you want a drink you have to go to the next town or elsewhere. Then, as a traveller, you can buy a drink.' This sounded like a very funny way of going on and I said so, asking what we should do. Tom replied sharp and to the point, 'It's Cardigan for us, my friend.'

We left camp at 7pm and started off towards Cardigan, about twelve miles away. On arrival we looked up a public house that Tom knew, and sampled the local brew. It was a very friendly place, and unfortunately I consumed a little more than I had ever previously drunk - two, maybe three pints. At closing time, we bid our new-found friends goodbye, and left to make our way back to camp.

There was no local transport so we were obliged to walk. It was cold, and the beer I had consumed was having a definite effect on me. So when we arrived at a telephone box in a village called Penparo, we stopped and entered the kiosk in the hope of warming ourselves up a bit.

For some reason we decided to sit on the floor. Not very clever, but we both fell asleep there. We woke up with a start, colder than ever, and decided to do Scouts' pace back to camp: twenty paces trotting, and twenty paces fast walking. This was good for the circulation and we began to feel good. Then came the shock. We were back in Cardigan!

Our subsequent journey back to Aberporth was slow and exhausting. We managed to get past the guardroom without being noticed, but it seemed only five minutes since we'd fallen asleep when reveille sounded. We dragged ourselves to the washroom, and got ourselves ready for the day ahead.

After completing the course of training at the firing camp, we left Aberporth on Thursday 11th January, 1940. We travelled by probably the same civilian lorries back to Newcastle Emlyn, and thence by train, once more through the night, arriving at Paddington Station at about five o'clock in the morning. Once again the Royal

Army Service Corps vehicles were waiting for us, and took us firstly to the Westminster Bank Sports Ground, and then to the Shirley Militia Camp, where I resumed my work as a Limber Gunner. Here life went on as before.

Battery Fitter

I was now really enjoying army life, and was glad to be able to avoid the everlasting round of fatigues, guard duties and drills. I also realised that, having managed to obtain one of the few plum jobs to be had, my next move was to convince my officers that they had made the correct choice in selecting me.

From my role as Limber Gunner, I progressed to become the Battery Fitter, with trade pay to supplement my meagre army pay. With this job came promises that I would be sent away on a number of courses to advance my knowledge of 'my gun'. My officers were very complimentary about my efforts and I was determined to make good progress.

On one occasion I had a bit of a scare: I had broken out in a strange rash and, bearing in mind what had happened over at Hayes Common when I was a dispatch rider, I made my first visit to the M.O. He took one look at me, laughed aloud and said, 'Bloody hell, German measles!'

After packing my kit, I was carted off to Croydon General Hospital, and spent a relaxed and almost enjoyable few days there. My only worry was that during my absence, someone might pick up my plum job as Battery Fitter. I need not have worried, for within a few days I was discharged and returned to my unit, where everyone said they hoped I was all right, and that they had missed me. I was very happy to return to my work, and glad that my efforts were appreciated.

In March, 1940, I was given a Late Pass until midnight. I arranged to meet my father at The Victoria Palace Theatre in London, where he had offered to take me to a show, but as I entered the theatre foyer, I found one of his officers waiting for me. There had been an assassination at Caxton Hall, Westminster, and the assassin, Mohamed Singh Azard - also known as Udham Singh - had travelled all the way from India with one object in mind: to commit this foul murder of Sir Michael O'Dwyer.

At this particular time, my father was the Divisional Detective Inspector in charge of the C.I.D., 'A' Division, of the London Metropolitan Police. His head station and office were at Cannon Row Police Station, just off Whitehall in Westminster. Needless to say, my father had urgent business to attend to that night, leaving me to see the show alone. I have no recollection now of that show; all my thoughts that night were with my father, imagining how he would be conducting the murder investigation.

The reason for this murder became obvious during the subsequent enquiries. The murderer's brother had been shot by British troops during the Amritsar Riots in India in 1919 as a direct result of Sir Michael confirming the order to the troops to fire on the mob. At that time, Sir Michael had been Governor of the province. For this murder, Udham Singh duly appeared at the Central Criminal Court in London (also known as the Old Bailey), was sentenced to death and later executed.

My fringe involvement in this incident fired up my enthusiasm to join the Police, to the extent that I followed the case through as far as I could from newspaper reports. This was definitely the work I wanted to become involved in later in life, when the war was over.

It was already very clear to most of us that the war was going to last for a few years yet. Those who had thought, back in 1939, that it would be over in six months had long since put that idea aside, for the reminders that the war was extending its clutches over Europe rather than withdrawing were ever present in those days.

PART TWO

On The Move

I became completely absorbed in my job as a Battery Fitter. My work basically entailed oiling, greasing and making sure that the guns were kept clean and in full working order. They were never fired, but used only for gun drill. However, nuts and bolts did sometimes work loose as the result of this, so checking the equipment was important.

At the same time, I felt somewhat guilty in my new role as Battery Fitter, where the only tools I had were those I had cadged from the Quartermaster or brought from home. Nevertheless, my work was appreciated by those I reported to, and that counted for a lot.

I carried on with my paid grease monkey work until 10th April, 1940, when I was sent for by the Battery Captain. He handed me a travel warrant to go to Letchworth in Hertfordshire, and told me to report to the Government Training Centre there.

Fitter Course at Letchworth

I was told that this was the Ascot Water Heater Works, that it was now closed, and that it was only a short walk from the railway station. As directed, I made my way to the G.T.C., and there I was greeted with open arms. The course started the following day, but I was first given an address to report to in Letchworth, and told that this would probably be my billet during the course. Furthermore, the people living there would be looking after me while I remained in Letchworth.

I went to the address and met the couple who were very pleased to be doing their bit for the war effort. There was another soldier in the house, Joe French, who came from Birmingham. He was also on the course and we became good friends. I explained to him that I was a wartime soldier, and had little engineering knowledge but was prepared to listen and learn. He was an engineer in peacetime, and had served in the Merchant Navy as a Fitter. Joe assured me that if I wanted to learn the trade, it would be easy, providing I concentrated on what was said during the course. He was very helpful.

The following morning, after a good breakfast, we made our way to the Ascot Factory, as we used to call it. There I met Jock Ogilvie, the instructor, a short stocky Scot with a very broad accent.

The Government Training Centre - Letchworth ~ 1940.

I was allocated a place on a bench next to Joe French, and given a few tools in the form of files, a hammer and some metal chisels. I was also given a piece of metal that was about eight inches long and one and a half inches wide, square in section. One side had been subjected to some pretty savage attacks and was all chipped. I was told to file that side flat. 'Now for the first time,' I was told 'you're going to find out what "file it flat" means.'

I set about the task in hand. This was my first attempt at accurate filing and try as I might I could not avoid a slight curve in the finish as I started and ended the push and draw with the file. Yet I felt I had done quite a good job, and along with others I took my piece of metal to the instructor.

When he came to my piece, Mr Ogilvie laid it on the bench face down, then picked up a chisel and proceeded to make a number of dents in the exposed face. 'You'll have to do better than that,' he said, putting the piece of metal on to a surface plate. He then proceeded to show me how it rocked, and explained that damp and dust would get into the space, causing rust and other elements to also get in.

I returned to my bench and sought advice from Joe. He looked at my piece of work and laughed. 'Filing flat is the most difficult job of all,' he said. 'Very few people can manage it, and you'll have to practise, practise, and practise again. It will come, but it takes time.' He then proceeded to watch my efforts, and stopped me to tell me that I was making the same mistake every time I pushed the file forward and drew it back. He then demonstrated just how to use the file, and again watched me closely until he was satisfied with my efforts.

Later that day, I took my piece back to Mr Ogilvie. 'Why didn't you do that the first time?' he asked. 'You did do this one, I hope?' I assured him that it was my own work, and he went on to tell me that actual filing was the most difficult thing to do in engineering. 'It's entirely up to you what shape your work will end up. Concentrate on what you're doing all of the time, and you'll be able to do it without difficulty. If you don't concentrate on your work, it will rock like it did the first time.' Then he threw my piece of metal into a bin and handed me a circular piece of metal about an inch across and a half inch thick. 'I want you to turn this into a three-eighths Whitworth nut. That'll keep you out of mischief tomorrow!'

It was now time to stop work and go back to our billets. Joe and I left together and I told him that making a nut out of such a piece of metal was something of a challenge. His answer was short and crisp: 'It may well be difficult,' he said, 'but if you do as I say it shouldn't give you any trouble at all'

As we made our way home, I told Joe that I had never used taps and dies, and was a little worried about the prospects. As far as he was concerned, however, using taps and dies was mostly a matter of pure common sense. He said that he would show me what to do in the morning, and was very firm about the fact that I must pay particular attention to the instructions about marking out the work. That, he said, was the most important job of all.

The following day I received my first lesson in marking out on metal, a most important job that had to be done accurately. Then Joe showed me how to use a centre square to mark the centre spot with a centre punch, to be drilled out later and tapped with the required Whitworth thread. With the small piece of metal in the vice, I proceeded under his eagle eye to file the hexagon for the nut. I did not do a bad job, but the finished article was not all that. When I was given the taps, Joe pointed out that three were required to do the job properly: the taper tap to start with, the secondary tap, and the plug tap to pass through the work to ensure that all swarfe was out.

Mr Ogilvie was happy with the Whitworth tapping, but passed some fairly caustic remarks about my efforts at filing the hexagon. Once again throwing my effort into the waste bin, he handed me another similar circular piece of metal and said, 'I want a proper job done tomorrow. This is an important task that you must learn properly, and one that you'll be called upon to do regularly.'

I'd had a very interesting week at the Ascot works, and felt happy with my progress, but I had begun to realise that the word 'practice' was one I would have to take seriously.

At midday on Saturday, we were dismissed for the weekend, and after returning to the billet and tidying myself up, I made my way to the railway station and got a train to Kings Cross. From there, I had to hack my way across London to my home in Norbury, south of the River Thames, nearly twenty miles away. By the time I got there, I felt that I would have to do something about getting a motorcycle for this journey, or I would be spending the whole weekend travelling.

My father was anxious to know how I had got on, and I explained to him the difficulties I'd had in filing. Never lost for an answer, Dad proceeded to tell me that, as I was a reasonable carpenter, there was no reason why I should not be fairly good with metal. 'You can plane and chisel straight and flat. Just concentrate, and practise. It'll come, you'll see.' I always accepted my father's advice as it had always been sound, but I was quite sure that this type of work was not as easy as he would have me believe.

I was unable to find myself a motorcycle, but the friends I approached said they would look round and see what was going. On the Sunday afternoon, I made my way back to Kings Cross, and thence to Letchworth and my billet, arriving at about eight o'clock in the evening. Joe and I were at the Ascot Factory at half past eight the following morning. The day's work ahead of us was in the blacksmith's shop, something I knew nothing about - in fact even less than I knew about doing something with a piece of metal and a file!

Our first lesson was to make a chain link and weld it together by heating it to an almost molten state, then hammering the ends together. When we were shown by the expert, it appeared so easy, but I was to learn that, like so many other facets of basic engineering, there was a lot more to it.

The best part of this week was spent on basic blacksmith work, coupled with that of the tinsmith. I questioned why this work should be done together, and was told that the blacksmith's main job was to fashion metal into shape, prior to perhaps welding or bolting it into position. The tinsmith, on the other hand, had to fashion lighter metal into shape and, by bending back the edges of the work, he was sometimes able to join work together and avoid the need for welding. The hood over the blacksmith's fire was given as an example of this fact. Most of this week was spent in the blacksmith's shop, and it was very interesting hot-riveting pieces of metal or sheet together, as well as setting up springs, a specialist job that was not taken lightly

The whole idea of setting up a spring was to get the metal to the right heat, and set it in the right shape when the colours appeared in the correct shade. It was a vital job which required a lot of practice to get it right.

At the end of this week, I needed to get home quickly. A message had been left for me from one of my old friends who had a Francis Barnet 125cc motorcycle for sale for £25. I would have to see this machine. My journey home was quite tedious, and I was hoping very much that I would be able to buy the bike and travel more easily to Letchworth in the future. I went to see it and immediately took a liking to it. I started it up, thankfully with ease, and then took it down the road and back. The engine sounded good, and I could not feel that anything was wrong with it. It was nothing like my old A.J.S. Silver Streak, but was in an entirely different class. There was no excess rust, and did everything I wanted. I even got the price down to £20, which was quite a bargain.

The log book and coupon for petrol was handed over, and I took the motorcycle home. The petrol allowance for this machine was so small that I was wondering whether it would pay me to use it on the trip back and forth to Letchworth. I mentioned this to my father. He had a small car but did not use it a lot, so he promised to help me out with petrol. I felt a little more secure.

Work at the Ascot Factory went on as before, with Mr Ogilvie always setting us one test or another. He was very helpful and patient with us. I became quite good with a file, and all went well until I saw what he wanted us to do for our final test. He produced a piece of metal three-eighths of an inch thick and told us to cut a piece from it that would finish up five inches by two-and-a-half inches, and dead square. We had to file three sides square with a file, the other side with a chisel.

Mr Ogilvie inspected our work and, finding it satisfactory, told us to drill two five-sixteenth holes in it, four and a quarter inches apart. Again we complied, but Mr Ogilvie's inspection rather shocked us this time. Thankfully Joe had advised me to be sure that I drilled the holes in the correct place, and marked out the metal accurately at first. 'There's a catch in this somewhere, John,' he said.

Mr Ogilvie produced a piece of metal with two spikes in it. The spikes were square to the base, and he offered this up to our test pieces. Many were rejected because the spikes would not go smoothly into the holes. Luckily, my piece passed muster and was given back to me together with some taps which I was to use to create a thread in each hole.

I had no difficulty in tapping the holes with these taps, and took my test piece back to Mr Ogilvie. After checking the threads, he gave me a drawing of a piece of metal with an egg-shaped hole in it. The exact sizes were shown on this drawing, and Mr Ogilvie calmly told me to cut out a hole in my test piece the same size as in the drawing. He then gave me a piece of metal three-and-a-half inches by one-and-a-half inches, and three-eighths of an inch thick. His final words were, 'Don't rush it, you have the rest of the week. That second piece of metal has got to fit four ways into the hole you make, and with no gaps more than five-thousandths of an inch.' As he said this he was brandishing a set of feeler gauges.

I was a little unhappy when I examined the drawing. This was quite a task, and I wanted so badly to pass the test. While I was reading through the drawing, Joe came over to me. 'What old Jock said to you is right, John. Take your time whatever you do, and if you're in doubt at all, give me a shout.'

I worked hard and cautiously throughout that week. Quite frankly, I doubted whether I would ever complete the task to the satisfaction of Mr Ogilvie.

After many hours of extreme concentration and not a little worry, I finally produced the finished article and proudly presented it to Mr Ogilvie. I felt I had done a good job, but at the same time I was not sure if it would be good enough. I certainly would not have wanted to make another similar article. To my surprise, our instructor complimented me. The old boy scratched his head and said, 'A good job, John. I didn't think you could do it.' I still have that test piece, and am looking at it as I type. I am still very proud of it, but doubt whether I could repeat what I did so many years ago.

Joe, some of the lads on the course and I met up on the Friday night, and went on quite a binge. There were some, however, who went to drown their sorrows because they had failed to pass out. I was certainly lucky, and most thankful to have Joe French to call on for advice when I needed it. The course had lasted until the middle of July, and I returned to the regiment happy in the thought that I knew my job. There was talk of many moves afoot, and the rumour-mongers were having a great time.

Gun Fitter Course at Woolwich

Nobody wanted to say anything to clarify the matter. Even the dispatch riders had nothing to say on the subject. But I didn't have to wait long to find out. Regimental Headquarters was going to move to Felixstowe, and 303 Battery would be moving over to the coast very soon. Then while I was pondering over all this, I was handed a Movement Order to go to Shrapnel Barracks in Woolwich, part of the Royal Artillery Barracks in that town, to take the Anti Aircraft Command Fitter Gun course. I was elated.

This was my first stay at a regular army barracks, and I soon learned the true meaning of army discipline. I also learned that this was not meant to be a rest camp. From our billet in the barracks I had to march, not walk, to the 'gun shop' (as we called it) about a quarter of a mile away. On that short journey, I found that I generally passed four or five officers, all of whom expected a smart salute. On my first trip to the gun shop, I was stopped by a very young Captain, who went to great pains to tell me that my uniform was scruffy and my boots were dirty.

His tirade of abuse continued. I should be ashamed of myself, he said, and had better learn to salute properly. In my ignorance of army ways, I attempted to make excuses, but this only added fuel to his verbosity. He was certainly overdoing it, and finally he dismissed me, telling me that he would be watching out for me in the future.

I mentioned this incident to one of the instructors in the gun shop. He gave me some fairly frank advice. Firstly, my boots had not been boned. The toe caps of soldiers' boots in Woolwich were expected to be highly polished. Furthermore, Battle Dress might not be as smart as Service Dress but at Woolwich, soldiers were expected to press their trousers and crease their jackets, as his were. I had never seen a Battle Dress jacket with so many creases in it. That night, I set to and spent the evening working on my boots and equipment. I was also shown how to bone my boots using a heated spoon.

It was now the middle of August, 1940, and air raids seemed to be the order of the day. Dog fights could often be observed up in the thirty thousand feet area, and my thoughts were that our guns must soon earn their keep. In the gun shop we had 3-, 3.7- and 4.5-inch guns, and others whose names I do not recall now. It was a most interesting course, with instructors who truly knew their business. We made notes, dismantled parts of guns, and answered questions by the score. Here I think I learned more about my charges, the 3-inch and 3.7-inch guns than I ever would have elsewhere. This course was run by people who really knew their job.

There was only one shock during my time here. We were paying strict attention as usual to an interesting talk when there was a terrific explosion nearby, with the noise of bits and pieces falling on to our roof. We went outside. There in the middle of the road I saw the tail of a Spitfire or Hurricane protruding from a large smoking hole. The pilot had not been seen to escape from his plane. There was nothing any of us could do but we all said a silent prayer for our now obviously departed comrade.

Finsbury Park Gun Site

The course ended on the 6th September, 1940, with written and practical examinations. Thankfully I passed, and felt that I had learned much that would be of considerable assistance to me in my trade as the war went on. I had been told that my unit had moved to the sports ground in Finsbury Park, North London, and made my way there.

To my surprise, I had been promoted to Full Bombardier while at Woolwich, and proudly donned my two stripes. I slept in a wooden hut that had been erected for the purpose, close to the sports ground. Each night there were heavy air raids, and I was often called out in the middle of the night to sort out problems.

On the sports ground, just inside the running track which circled the ground, was a Nissen hut which was used to store ammunition. Here I made up a bench for my work, and laid out the few tools I had. I was unhappy about the hut I slept in, because shrapnel nearly came through the roof one night. I therefore decided, in my dubious wisdom, to sleep on top of the ammunition. I was happy in the thought that if the ammunition went up, it would have made such an explosion that my little wooden hut just over the road would have disappeared as well. I slept very soundly, so soundly in fact that the shrapnel which clattered down on the roof during the air raids did not worry me. I also found that I was not called out so many times now that I slept on top of the ammunition. I wonder why?

In October, we moved to Seckford Hall near Woodbridge in Suffolk, a beautiful house that we were told belonged to an Indian Army Colonel. The lighting here was by carbide lamps. There was a carbide generator which provided some very bright lighting throughout the building, and a number of gun sites near us which I had to visit from day to day to ensure that all was well. While here, I was promoted to Lance Sergeant, and had the dubious honour of being able to eat and drink in the Sergeants' Mess. It certainly had its good points and I was very happy.

But the good life here was soon to come to an end. I was suddenly moved with the Battery Headquarters contingent to nearby R.A.F. Wattisham.

R.A.F. Wattisham

At Wattisham, we were billeted in what in peacetime were married quarters for R.A.F. personnel. I found myself sharing a room with Battery Sergeant Major Giles and the Quartermaster Sergeant. Not a bad life; we actually had beds! There was the added bonus that we messed with the R.A.F. Sergeants, and they ate and drank well. They certainly earned it. The planes here were for the most part Blenheim Bombers.

The R.A.F. members of the mess were young, not much older than me. They were proud of their vocation, despite the fact that fatalities were all too many. During my short stay here I got to know one or two of these Air Crew members well. It was not too long, however, before the facts of R.A.F. life were brought home to me in a very direct and personal manner.

I had sat next to and drunk with one particular Sergeant pilot, whom I shall call George, on a couple of occasions, and we got on well. Then, one morning at breakfast, I asked another Sergeant where George was. The normally noisy mess went deadly silent.

My friend looked over and quietly said, 'He won't be back, John, he got hit over Cologne last night.' I was shocked, but could only offer sympathy, for what that was worth. Thereafter I did not

Lance Sergeant Swain ~ 1941.

enquire after those who did not turn up for breakfast, and many did not.

One morning, there was a general alarm. A Dornier Bomber had flown into the aerodrome area, dropped a bomb on one of the buildings and made off. The question put to me was understandable: 'What the hell are you lot going to do about that? That blighter has been here before, and will be back.' I returned to our billet with Sergeant Major Giles. On the way, he said to me, 'What's this I hear about you intending to go into the Police Force when this lot is over?'

'That's right, Sir,' I replied.

'Good,' came his reply, 'then I have a job for you.'

My first thoughts were, 'Christ, what have I volunteered for now?' and these remained with me until we reached our destination.

Back in the billet, the Sergeant Major continued. 'McDonald has gone over the side, John.' Exactly what that meant I was not sure. Was it desertion? A terrible word. Did it mean absent without leave? Not so bad, but still a crime by army standards. Just what was the Sergeant Major up to?

It so happened that when I joined the regiment at the end of August,1939, one of those who had joined the same day had been McDonald. He told me he had served in the Spanish Civil War, and he certainly did know quite a lot about army life. He was a lot older than me but we had got on well together.

My thoughts were cut short by the Sergeant Major saying to me, 'Take Gunner Bill Robson with you. I think he was supposed to have been a Special Constable or something like that. McDonald is being detained at Great Scotland Yard by the Military Police. You are now also the Battery Provost Sergeant, but there's no extra pay with it. You get enough as the Battery Fitter.'

The Interview with Colonel Imrie RCMP

The Sergeant Major handed me his revolver and said, 'Here, take this, you'll need it, and if he runs off, shoot him. He's a bloody deserter as far as I'm concerned.' I saw that the revolver was loaded, and strapped it on. I had never worn a pistol before, and certainly had never fired one. After I'd located Bill Robson, we were taken to Ipswich railway station, where we caught a train to London. On the way I turned over in my mind everything that Sergeant Major Giles had said to me.

Charlie Giles was the Battery Sergeant Major, and an experienced soldier. He had served some years in the Territorial Army, and had previously served as a regular soldier in the Welsh Guards. He had one medal, the soldiers' long service and good conduct medal, sometimes referred to as the pontoon medal, because a soldier had to serve at least twenty-one years to qualify for it. In the regiment, however, it was often called 'the mark of the beast', a name that probably referred to the Sergeant Major's terrible temper, which had left many of us shuddering at times.

As Bill Robson and I travelled on, I turned over in my mind the orders he had given me. I could not shake off my thoughts about his medal and my orders. I could not imagine myself shooting McDonald. It just did not make sense. Shoot an enemy, yes, but McDonald? Perhaps this 'mark of the beast' business was right. I would have to sort this order out, probably when we got back to camp, but there was going to be no shooting; I had made my mind up about that.

There was no time set for our return, and upon arriving at Liverpool Street Station, Bill and I found that there were plenty of trains going back to Ipswich later in the day. With the Sergeant Major's warning that I might have to take a shot at McDonald still very much in my mind, I felt this would be an ideal time for me to call on my father. His office was at Cannon Row Police Station, just off Whitehall and only a couple of hundred yards from Great Scotland Yard where McDonald was being held.

We made our way to Cannon Row Police Station. The entrance was sandbagged up and an officer was on guard. I explained that I was Divisional Detective Inspector Swain's son, and wanted to see him. After clearing my request, we went into the Police Station and were both taken to my father's office.

He was delighted to see me, and asked what I was doing in town. Proudly I told him that, in addition to being the Gun Fitter for the Battery, I was also the Provost Sergeant; further, that I had been sent to London to collect a deserter, McDonald, from Great Scotland Yard Military Police Barracks. Dad seemed impressed, but he was not the Divisional Detective Inspector for nothing. 'Do you always carry a revolver?' he asked.

'Of course,' I replied. Dad took the matter no further. He made a telephone call and arranged to meet someone for lunch. We walked out of Cannon Row and along Whitehall to Great Scotland Yard.

When we arrived, my father told the guard that we were there to see Colonel Imrie. We were ushered into the colonel's office. My father walked over to the Colonel as Robson and I stood smartly to attention and saluted. They talked quietly for a few minutes. Dad then looked towards us and pointing to me said to the Colonel, 'What do you think of him?'

The Colonel looked puzzled. 'Why?' he asked.

'He's my son,' father replied. The Colonel said that this was a great pleasure, and walked round his desk to come over to us and shake us by the hand. I thought the Colonel was about the smartest senior officer I had ever seen. His uniform fitted perfectly, and his two rows of medal ribbons were clear proof of his considerable military service. Furthermore, his greeting to two pretty obvious 'rookies' exuded a warmth of welcome that surprised and impressed us, coming as it did from one so senior.

My thoughts were interrupted by my father saying, 'I hope it *is* a pleasure; he's come to collect a prisoner you're holding.' Then, turning to me and pointing to my pistol, my father said, 'Tell the Colonel your instructions.'

I had no idea just what I had let myself in for. I knew my instructions, although I did not like them; I had purposely gone to see my father to get some guidance on just that subject. Furthermore, I was somewhat pleased, even smug about the fact that it was he who had picked upon the revolver, and I had not been obliged to put the question to him.

While these thoughts were going through my mind, I noticed that Colonel Imrie's whole attitude towards my colleague and me had changed, even hardened. Those calm and even kindly eyes that had greeted us a few minutes ago were now frighteningly sharp and I felt uneasy.

The change reminded me so much of the sudden change of attitude in R.S.M. Flemming back in August, 1939, when I told him that I thought I had joined the Royal Army Service Corps. I told the Colonel exactly what the Battery Sergeant Major had told me - that I was to shoot McDonald if he escaped from me.

'Are you quite sure of those instructions?' he asked.

'Quite sure, Sir,' I replied.

'Show me the pistol,' he said. I took the pistol from my holster, reversed it and handed it to him, butt first. He took it from me, tipped the bullets onto his desk, then put the pistol and bullets into his desk drawer and locked it. Looking me square in the eye, he said, 'If your Sergeant Major wants his pistol back, he'll have to collect it from here himself.' With that he thumped the desk with his fist.

From Great Scotland Yard, the four of us went to a nearby public house where we each had a pint of beer and some sandwiches. Dad returned to his duties, while my colleague and I returned with the Colonel to the Military Police Barracks.

Once in the Colonel's office, we were invited to take a seat and he proceeded to enlarge on our very limited military knowledge. He told us about an incident that had taken place a few weeks earlier. An escort had collected a prisoner from Great Scotland Yard but within a short distance, the prisoner had escaped and run off in Whitehall. One of the escorts, feeling that they were unable to recapture their man, drew his pistol and fired at him. The escort missed the escaping prisoner and hit an innocent civilian who just happened to be passing. The civilian was seriously injured, and the two soldiers comprising the escort were now facing Courts Martial and would undoubtedly be severely punished.

'Escorts,' the Colonel continued, 'may only fire at escaping prisoners of war if there is no other way of recapturing them and, most important of all, if the zone of fire is clear. Please remember that, gentlemen!' He then pressed the buzzer under his desk, and a military policeman came into the office. 'They've come for McDonald,' the Colonel said.

We were taken to the cells, where we signed for McDonald. I took the opportunity of having a short talk with him, warning him of the consequences of any attempt to escape. I felt sure that I had got my message over to our prisoner, and we made our way to the exit, where we were stopped by two military police officers.

'The Colonel wants to see you,' said the Sergeant. We were both taken to the Colonel's office.

'For your information,' the Colonel said, 'McDonald is a fool, but a very brave fool indeed. He overstayed his leave and, as far as we know, he was on his way back to his unit when a bomb dropped near him. A building was demolished, and he took it upon himself to jump in and pull out the occupants. He worked through the day and well into the night with the police and firemen. In the early hours of the morning, the search for further occupants was called off, and the police officers invited him back to Paddington Police Station to have a meal and a rest. This he declined. The Police, however, were not taking no for an answer, and took him back to the Police Station.

'This was undoubtedly so that they could contact his unit and tell them what had happened. On making their enquiries, however, they learned that he had been absent without leave for a number of days, and were asked to detain him. He will no doubt be charged with that offence, but the officers at Paddington Police Station have stated that they will attend any hearing there is to speak for this soldier and state exactly what he did. He may finish up in the glasshouse [military prison], he may not. That's all.'

I saluted and turned to leave. 'Just a minute,' said the Colonel. Turning back, I saw that he had Sergeant Major Giles' pistol in his hand. 'You'd better give this back to your Sergeant Major, but tell him exactly what I've told you. Also, if he wants his bullets back, he'll have to come here and collect them himself. If he dares.' Those last few words were said with such force that I felt quite sure our friendly Colonel was an adversary not to cross under any circumstances.

Leaving Great Scotland Yard, Robson, McDonald and I travelled to Ipswich from Liverpool Street Station. I was deep in thought over the happenings back in London. Knowing Robson had been a Special Constable before the war, I asked him what he thought about what had taken place at the Military Police Depot. He replied that it was a lesson well learned; at the same time, he would not like to be in my shoes when I told Charlie Giles that the Colonel had kept the ammunition from his pistol.

Robson was right. The Battery Sergeant Major was hopping mad. He ranted and raved for about ten minutes. Fancy telling a Colonel of the Military Police that your Sergeant Major had told you to shoot McDonald if he ran off! I was a new brand of idiot that had joined the army to avoid conscription, just because there was a war on. Frankly, he had me a little worried. I could see me landing up in the guardroom, directed to some horrible military chore, just to please him. I could even have blown my job as Battery Fitter.

There were many who wanted to step into that pleasant job and get away from the normal run of military routine. The more the Sergeant Major went on about my shortcomings, the more I felt that he realised the Colonel was right. Slowly, very slowly, he simmered down, then quite out of the blue, he said he thought that it was time he bought Robson and me a drink. Robson, who had been standing beside me during this time, was as surprised as I was, for during our very short time in the army, we had never seen Charlie Giles buy a drink. He seemed to be one of the lucky ones. Whenever he entered the canteen, there was always someone who wanted to do the honours and buy him a drink. This time, he was going to pay, and pay well for the wigging he had let loose on me earlier.

On my return to regimental duties, a further shock awaited me on my first morning back at Wattisham. The guns were all on stand-by, waiting for that damned Dornier that had made regular unwanted calls on us. Sure enough, from the gun site on the far side of the airfield, I heard the noise of an approaching plane flying low. It was eleven o'clock in the morning. It had to be that Dornier. The guns turned in the direction of the sound, and I saw the nose of the plane as the command to fire was given. It was an R.A.F. Baufort Bomber, and a hasty shout of 'Cease fiire!' was given, but all too late. The first single shot took off the lowered landing gear and parts of the undercarriage, then the plane pancaked on to the runway. Needless to say, the wires were red hot thereafter. The plane had been flown by a senior officer from Wattisham, who had been on an official visit to another R.A.F. Station. The trouble was that he had given no warning of his impending approach, in accordance with the very strict regulations at the time.

Of course, on the gun site, no-one knew about this, and we attempted to find out who was to blame. On my lunchtime visit to the Sergeants' Mess, however, a different story came out. The truth was that the army could not be blamed for the unannounced entrance of the plane.

We Move To Orkney

We were profoundly thankful for the fact that it was only our 3-inch guns that had fired. Had the plane flown over the 3.7-inch guns the result would have been far more serious.

In January, 1941, the Regiment moved off to the Orkney Islands. Regimental Headquarters, most of 303 Battery, and Battery Headquarters were based on South Ronaldsay in the area of Herston Point. We were involved in the defence of that great naval base, Scapa Flow, defence directed primarily against the probability of attacks from the air, but with an eye also towards the sea.

Our position was about seven miles from the only town on the island, St. Margaret's Hope. We also had guns on the islands of Burray and Flotta. The sinking of the British battleship, Royal Oak, by an enemy submarine had really stirred up the authorities who, in their misguided wisdom, had thought such an action was impossible.

Security was tight, and there was the general feeling that such an incident must never be allowed to happen again. Here small arms were looked upon as far more important weapons than on the English mainland, and we had the feeling that we were truly in the war, not just at the receiving end of the German Bombers' missiles.

One good thing that happened shortly after my arrival on Orkney was that I received two hundred Silk Cut cigarettes from my old employer, The Co-operative Wholesale Society. I thought that they had forgotten me, but need not have worried. In fact, throughout the war years I received this number of cigarettes every month, whenever I was on what was then classified as an overseas posting. My faith in the old firm and the security of my peacetime job - should I fail to get into the Police Force after the war - seemed to be assured.

Even while on Orkney, I was still secretly stunned by the lecture I had received from Colonel Imrie. I was also very much aware of the fact that I had never fired a pistol, even though I was regarded as the provost Sergeant. These thoughts haunted me regularly, particularly when it came to collecting prisoners, and I was involved in that task on a number of occasions. It always seemed pretty silly to me that I should have to carry a pistol, but had never had a chance to fire one on a range. I was due for quite a shock.

I built a rifle range for the instruction of the troops, and also for some of the naval personnel in the area who, like ourselves, were wartime volunteers. I was a fairly good shot with a rifle, and spent many hours training them in the use of the rifle. Now I had to borrow a pistol.

The Battery Sergeant Major was not at all keen to lend me his, despite the fact that it was his weapon that I used to have to wear on escort duty. Finally, and with some reluctance, he brought his pistol to the range, together with a box of ammunition. He also ordered me to bring a newly painted fire bucket, which he handed to me.

At the range he took the fire bucket from me and threw it on to the range area. It landed about twelve feet away. Then, taking his pistol from his holster, he handed it to me and pointed to the fire bucket. 'Hit that,' he said. Noticing my hesitation, he nudged me and said, 'Go on, fire one shot, hit it.' I took aim and fired. I missed the bucket by about a yard. 'Try again,' he ordered. I did, but the result was about the same. He took the pistol from me. 'Your Red Cap Colonel was right,' he said. 'That fellow certainly knew what he was talking about. The only thing he forgot to tell you was that a .45 pistol is not the most accurate of pistols, the .38 is far more accurate. But for now we'll have another go with this one.'

The result was that, with quite a lot of practice and guidance from the Sergeant Major, I became quite an acceptable shot with the pistol. I well remember his favourite catch phrase about pistol-shooting. 'Few people can hit a bloody barn door with a pistol, they're too impressed by what they see cowboys do on the pictures. It's not as easy as it seems.' He was right, of course.

The travel arrangements in Orkney were somewhat different from those I had previously been used to. From the port of St. Margaret's Hope, I was often required to travel to other islands in the course of my duties as Battery Fitter or Provost Sergeant. I often had to go to Burray, Flotta or Lyness on the main island of Orkney by drifter. A drifter, in military terminology, was a large fishing boat which had been taken into military or naval service to transport servicemen and civilians from island to island.

There were no creature comforts, in fact most of the people travelled in the hold of these boats, and were happy to do so. They were, however, very efficient and the skippers were generally the owners of the vessels. In rough seas they certainly bobbed about, and on many occasions the passengers were secured in the hold during the journey, with the hatch cover battened down. It was quite an experience, sitting in the semi-darkness listening to the water gushing overhead when the drifter cut through heavy seas.

As landlubbers, we were always to a man thankful that the skippers, generally tough-looking Orkadians, undoubtedly knew their job thoroughly. At Lyness the visit was usually to catch the larger ship that would take us over the Pentland Firth to Scrabster, the port for Thurso on the Scottish mainland. We would board either the St Ninian, quite a sizeable ship that had been many years on the Australian run from the U.K., or a second ship, the Marialta. Until we arrived at Lyness we rarely knew which ship was available.

It was generally on escort trips that I took the ferry to Scotland. From Scrabster, we would be taken to a transit camp just outside Thurso and remain there until just before the train left. This was generally at 6.30pm. On one occasion, I was going to York to pick up our old friend McDonald once again when I decided to call at the local Police Station in Thurso. The object of the exercise was to borrow some handcuffs; I had been told that I should be in possession of these when collecting McDonald from the York Detention Centre.

I did not intend to lose McDonald, and consequently my soft number as the Provost Sergeant. On the way back from York to Thurso, we would undoubtedly sleep at some time during the journey, and I intended to be prepared for any escape attempts.

Travelling on the 6.30pm train from Thurso was always a lot of fun. The train was nicknamed 'the Jellico' by the troops; don't ask me why. Personally I felt that if it were to have a name, 'the Jericho' would have been nearer the mark, because the noise of jollification in it on occasions was surely sufficient to make the walls of that ancient city come tumbling down. It was always a happy train, for the passengers, almost to a man, were from one or other of the armed services, either on leave and travelling home to their loved ones, or on the move away from the desolation of the islands.

At the York Detention Centre, Robson and I took charge of McDonald, where everything was done in double march time. We were rather surprised, and so was McDonald. On our way to the railway station, holding up his handcuffed hand he said, 'I thought we were friends.'

'Yes, Mac, I replied, 'we are friends, but in these circumstances, I have a job to do, and this is as it has to be.' He soon obviously resigned himself to his position, and relaxed for the journey back to camp.

At Thurso we were taken by army lorry to the dock at Scrabster, and there I handed the handcuffs back to the local Police. Once on board St. Ninian and past the shelter of Dunnet Head, we soon learned just how cruel the sea can be.

The Pentland Firth was at its best, or perhaps I should say at its worst. I had never been on a fairly large ship before that just ploughed through waves as high as the bridge; in fact the St Ninian and the Marialta were the largest ships I had ever been on.

Certainly this was the worst sea I had ever seen up to this time. The noise was just deafening, and although I was not seasick, I was not the only one who was far from happy. I was just amazed that the ship remained in one piece above water in the face of such a buffeting. A voice beside us brought me out of my thoughts of the terror. It was an old Naval Petty Officer, wearing ribbons from an earlier war. 'Don't worry, Sarge,' he said, 'it's often like this, and this bloody ship has been doing this run for the past fourteen years without mishap.

Personally, I wanted to lie down somewhere away from the noise and crashing of the ship into huge waves, but I had to stay with my charge. We had returned the handcuffs and, knowing McDonald as I did, I was sure he was the sort of chap who would jump overboard, just for the hell of it. We took our prisoner back to camp without incident, but the journey from Scrabster to Lyness, which normally took four hours, took nine on this occasion. Quite frankly we were all positively relieved to get our feet back on dry land.

The island of South Ronaldsay and our location at Herston Point had a rugged fascination for me. There was an abundance of rabbits which I managed to shoot occasionally for the benefit of the Sergeants' Mess. There were also the thousands of seagulls which, when the time was right, obliged us by laying a lot of eggs. The Sergeants' Mess, thanks to the work behind the scenes by the Mess Cook, ate a good portion of omelettes made from these eggs. They had a slightly fishy taste, but with the aid of some issue brown sauce, it was hardly noticed and never complained of.

My travels between the islands to carry out small repairs were most interesting. We passed groups of 'block ships' - ships that had been sunk in gaps between the islands to prevent foreign unauthorised ships from getting into Scapa Flow unnoticed. I also made friends with local crofters and found their way of life most interesting. During these journeys, I often saw many dolphins. They seemed to love following the drifters on fine days. They are such beautiful animals, and I am glad to say I have never caught a dolphin, or seen one on a fishmonger's slab.

I had no desire to catch dolphins but fancied doing some fishing, although I did not know where to start in Orkney. Just below our camp at Herston Point, there was a croft virtually on the seashore. It was also on the edge of a rock-strewn field where there were some sheep. One day I decided to pay a call on the croft. I knocked at the door, asked for the man of the house, and was told he was not well. I was, however, invited in.

Sitting in a rather crude chair that had seen better days was Tom Cussiter, and from the first moment of introduction, we became firm friends. It was June, a month when the best fishing was available, and he could not get out because he could not get his boat down the beach to the sea outside his house. I told him that I would help him, and his eyes brightened immediately. 'We've only got two weeks of saith left,' he said. 'If you could help me get the boat down to the water, we'll start whenever you can come down.' Then as an afterthought, he asked, 'Can you row a boat?'

I assured him that I could, although I had never in my life rowed such a large craft as I had seen outside the croft. Nevertheless, I felt happy, because rowing is rowing, and I was fairly fit and strong in those days. I asked if he had plenty of fishing tackle and he assured me that he thought he had enough for that year, and would show it to me when I next came down. We had a cup of tea together and after that I returned to camp. On the way back, however, it suddenly occurred to me that he had mentioned saith. I had heard of these fish somewhere, but could not connect them with any fish that I knew.

The month of June in Orkney is very special. The fishing is at its best, and I have even read a book at two o'clock in the morning in the open air, without artificial light, thanks to the Northern Lights, or *Aurora Borialis*.

The following evening, I went down to Tom Cussiter's croft. He was in his shed examining his fishing lines, removing some very rusty hooks and replacing them. To these long-shanked hooks he was tying some pieces of white gull feather. His fishing rods were sixteen-foot lengths of cane with a length of heavy line attached. The first six feet of line was made from heavy gut, to which he attached four or five of the long shanked hooks. Each had a small piece of gull feather tied to it in a shape similar to a large white fly. Where the gut joined the line, there was a piece of lead twisted and pinched round the line.

We placed the rods in the boat and between us, including Mrs Cussiter, we pushed the craft down the stoney beach into the sea. Once in there, I took up the oars and began to row. This was a lot different from rowing a boat on the River Thames! It was hard work, damned hard work, and Tom Cussiter watched me very intently for a while. He finally relaxed his watch, and I felt satisfied that I had at least given him a little assurance of my ability.

The croft was situated on the beach of a sound, a sheltered expanse of water lying behind Herston Point. Once in the middle of the sound, Tom placed the rods in the prepared grooves in the transom and let the lines trail away to the rear. He then turned to give me directions to steer into the open sea.

Suddenly one of the rods started to bend and shake. Tom hauled it clean out of the water, and shook what looked like a nice-sized pollock on to the floor of the boat. He immediately returned the rod to the groove, and the line trailed away behind us again.

Pointing at the fish, Tom announced, 'That's a sillock.' It weighed about a pound, and to me it was a small pollock, if I had ever seen one on a fishmonger's slab. However, I was not going to argue with him; he undoubtedly knew what he was talking about. Tom was in a talkative mood, and I learned a lot about these fish with strange names. Though I was still convinced that they were all of the pollock family, probably in various stages of their growth and development, I discovered that here on Orkney, they were known as either peltecks, sillock, saith or lye. I had never heard of these names before, with the exception of saith. They were all shaped the same, but differed slightly in colour.

The pelteck was the smallest and very silvery; the sillock was slightly larger and pinkish. Both weighed up to a pound. Saith were reddish-brown in colour, and weighed up to about two-and-a-half pounds. The lye were lightish brown, and came in at three pounds and over.

The rods continued to flutter and shake, while I just sat and slowly rowed the boat onwards. Tom drew in the lines and shook off the fish on to the bottom of the boat. We had quite a haul, it was fascinating. It was also rather a massacre, and I was wondering just what he would do with all the fish.

Suddenly, Tom looked at his watch and called over to me, 'We have to go now.' I started to turn the craft and row back towards the croft. Then I heard the motors of a naval motor torpedo boat that was anchored in the sound start up. I rowed back to the croft, then with the assistance of Mrs Cussiter, we hauled the boat up the beach to leave it above the tide waterline.

Once the boat was secured, I assisted Tom to carry the haul to his shed. During the evening, we had caught over a hundredweight of fish. I put aside a dozen for the M.T.B. crew, and took a dozen back to the Sergeants' Mess where we had quite a feast of fresh fish prepared by the Mess Cook and a good time was had by all.

I returned to Tom's croft the following day, and we repeated the exercise. Before going into the open sea, however, I took the boat over to the M.T.B. and handed the crew some of the fish we had caught the previous day, which had been kept for them on a slab in Tom Cussiter's shed. Santa Claus would not have had a better reception. The fish were gratefully received, and we were plied with cigarettes and tobacco, well above the standard that we could have purchased either in the Sergeants' Mess, or in St. Margaret's Hope. The first words of the crew were, 'Just bring them over whenever you like, and thanks a million.' We caught fish again in exactly the same manner as on the previous day, and returned before the M.T.B. went out on patrol. We again passed over to our naval friends a little something to supplement their rations.

The barter was good, and was well appreciated all round. During a period of nearly a year on South Ronaldsay, I went out with Tom Cussiter on many occasions. The fish, however, were never so plentiful as they were in that wonderful month of June, when it did not seem to get dark until nearly four in the morning, thanks to the Northern Lights. As for the amount of fish that were placed in Tom's shed, none was wasted. Those he did not eat or give away were salted down in the island way with sea salt, to be eaten later in the year. I was, as you will appreciate, thoroughly enjoying life in the army, and as a fisherman.

On one of my trips to Tom Cussiter's croft, I found him in his shed cleaning a large rifle that looked more like an anti-tank rifle than a shotgun. This was very interesting. As I recall it now, this weapon was about five feet in length overall, and had a bore somewhere in the region of one-and-a-half inches. I was rather fascinated by the two spigots that protruded from the side of the rifle at the centre of gravity point.

These spigots formed what in artillery terms would be referred to as part of the trunion. This was a very large shotgun indeed. Certainly it could never be carried and fired from the shoulder, and it was not made to be. Indicating the spigots, I questioned Tom on this point. From the corner of his shed he produced a heavy pole about the same length as the gun, and some three inches in diameter. At one end of this pole there was a brass casting which formed a double fork to take the spigot. We now had a complete trunion. At the opposite end of the pole there was a brass ferrule fitted.

The gun was very heavy indeed, but I do not now recall any of the particulars of the writing and engraving upon it. As for the method of projection, it used a charge of black powder and an ignition cap. The powder would be poured down the barrel from a purpose-made container. A wad of what looked like compressed cardboard would then be rammed down on top of the powder and lead shot would be poured down the barrel, then a further wad rammed down on top of the pellets or shot.

Tom continued his explanation. The pole was passed through a hole in the centre seat of the boat, and into a retainer secured to the planking and bearers at the bottom of the craft. Now the gun was placed on the pole and a strap secured round the butt to keep it upright. Then, if it was raining and likely to be used, a waterproof cap was placed over the muzzle. This seemed to be a task that took quite a while to complete, and I told Tom so.

His reply had me laughing. He usually went out just before dawn with his pre-loaded 'duck gun', as he called it, strapped to the pole. He secured it in the centre of the rowing boat and would then row to a marshy patch below a hill by his croft and wait for the ducks to fly over. From experience, he had found that the ducks usually flew over just before dawn, generally in a flock of between twenty and fifty. He would only fire one shot, for he was not interested in firing at single birds, and there was generally only one flock to consider. He ended his dissertation by explaining that he was cleaning up his gun because it was the time when the flocks would be moving around, and asked whether I wanted to come along with him on his next visit. Needless to say, I just had to see what happened, and although I was not in the habit of getting up in the middle of the night, I felt that this was something I would make an exception for.

Within a few days of that unusual visit, I went to Tom's croft at four in the morning. He and his wife were waiting for me. We fixed the pole in the centre of the rowing boat, then strapped the gun in position. After that we pushed the boat into the sea and got in ourselves. I rowed the boat over to the M.T.B. and Tom called over to the sentry on watch that we were going to 'have a look' at some ducks. The sentry laughed and said, 'OK, but don't forget us.'

I then rowed on for about a half hour until we grounded in some reeds. Tom cocked the gun, took off the muzzle cover and placed an ignition cap on the anvil under the hammer. It was now a matter of waiting. We were both well wrapped up and settled down, having lit our pipes, to await the pleasure of the ducks.

Suddenly Tom was alert. He didn't say a word, but I saw his shoulders hunch up a little as he took hold of the gun and pointed it at the brow of the hill above us. I could hear nothing, then a pair of ducks flew over. Tom lifted his hand with a single finger extended. I took this as an indication to keep quiet while the birds flew over us. Then a large flock appeared from over the hill. There must have been fifty or more there. I was watching the flock and the movement of the gun muzzle when it suddenly erupted.

There was a very loud roar, an orange flash, and the boat moved suddenly about four feet back into the reeds. We had some difficulty propelling it out of the reeds, then set about recovering the ducks. We gave two to the M.T.B. crew, two to the Sergeants' Mess, and Tom attended to the remainder. Quite an experience!

My fishing had now come to an end, however, which had happened quite suddenly. With the fishing at an end, I settled down to my Battery duties, and visits to various crofts on South Ronaldsay. It was a pleasant and comparatively easy life, and I got on well with the officers and men. The Admin Officer for 303 Battery was Captain Dilwyn John.

The Military College of Science

Captain John was a thorough gentleman, and I was never happy with the nickname that the lads of the Battery had christened him with: 'the Chinese laundry man.' When I enquired as to the reasons for this, I was assured that it was in no way meant to be offensive. He was a man that no man would give offence to. Very few members of the Battery had a medal; Captain John was one of the few. He had one medal, the Polar Medal, which was white, and he had earned it with Captain Scott on his Antarctic expeditions after travelling with him on one of his Polar explorations.

One morning shortly after my early morning outing with Tom Cussiter and his duck gun, I was walking towards my workshop when I heard a call from the Battery Sergeant Major: 'Sergeant Swain, cuuuurm 'eeeeer!' I spun round. It was so unlike Charlie Giles to call me in such a manner. I marched over to him and stood to attention. 'Captain John wants to see you,' he said. 'You'd better get over there straight away.'

'Right, Sir,' I said, and marched off. I did not come into contact with Captain John very often because my work came under the Technical Officer, Captain Griffiths. On this particular occasion, however, it was Captain John who had sent for me, and as I walked towards his office my mind was in something of a turmoil. What had I done? I kept asking myself. Had I forgotten something important and upset the officers? I could think of nothing that might have upset them, although perhaps it was the fishing trips and the duck shoot.

I knocked on Captain John's door and marched in. It was January, 1942, and Captain John was full of my praises. I had done a good job of work and he would be sorry to lose me. Lose me? What the devil was going on? I could not work this one out at all. He continued: 'There's a chance for you to go to the Military College of Science. We will be sorry to lose you.' There, he had said it again. I had no intention of leaving the Regiment, and told him so in as firm and polite a manner as possible under the circumstances. 'Go away and think about it,' he said. I saluted and left the office, but as far as I was concerned, there was nothing to think about.

On my way back to my workshop, that voice cut through the air once again. 'Sergeant Swain, cuuurm 'eeer!' Yes, it was Battery Sergeant Major Giles once again. This time everyone stopped in their tracks and turned round, including me. I marched over to him once again, stopped smartly in front of him and said, 'Sir?'

'Captain Griffiths wants you,' he said. 'Take my advice, young soldier: take his, you'll be a bloody fool if you don't.' With that I was marched into Captain Griffiths' office by the Sergeant Major, which of itself was most unusual. I had always got on well with Captain Griffiths; I trusted him and respected his judgement. I also felt that he had a certain respect and feeling for me, young as I was in those days.

He looked at me steadily, and then said, 'Captain John saw you just now and you had some doubts about his offer, I'm told. Well, this is the situation: here is your Movement Order to the Military College of Science at Stoke on Trent, and here is your Travel Warrant.'

I accepted these documents. Then looking me in the eye quite sternly, the Captain said, 'You're not going to turn me down, John, are you?'

'No, Sir,' I replied.

'Then pack your kit. You leave this morning. You don't realise just how important this move is to you.' With that he reached over to me, hand outstretched. We shook hands and he wished me good luck. I saluted, turned and left his office.

I have to admit that it was with a certain amount of sadness that I left the London Welsh Regiment. I had been very happy in my work, I had learned so much and got on well with everyone. As I looked back from the truck that took me off to St. Margaret's Hope, I found myself wondering whether I would ever rejoin or see my old comrades again, or if I would ever have the opportunity to ramble over that rugged scenery that had impressed me so much.

At St. Margaret's Hope, I caught the drifter to Flotta. I was now on my way to a part of England that I had never visited before, making one of my last trips in one of the drifters that I had grown to love travelling in so much. At Flotta, I had to transfer to another drifter to take me to Lyness. There, with my kit, I climbed the ladder to the jetty without difficulty, and succeeded in boarding the St. Ninian at Lyness. Once there I settled down to enjoy the trip across the now calm Pentland Firth.

I kept thinking how glad I was that I had not had to carry my tools with me when I'd travelled to the various islands to do repairs for the Regiment. There had always been sufficient tools on each gun site. Thus I had not experienced the difficulties of carrying heavy loads up and down ladders, especially as, more often than not, the drifters were being moved around by rough seas.

It was the most pleasant journey I had ever experienced, going over the Pentland Firth to Scrabster. The gannets at Dunnet Head were having a field day diving for fish. It was quite a sight.

From the dock at Scrabster, I was taken with others, most of whom were going home on leave, to the transit camp. There, after a short period in the canteen, most of us were moved off to the railway station at Thurso. I boarded 'the Jellico' at 6.30pm, and after drinking a bottle of beer and eating some sandwiches, I fell asleep.

I was woken up by the noise of the train as we passed along the gully between the built-up railway embankments of the single line track near Strathpeffer. There was plenty of singing on the train; obviously there was something of a party going on in one of the carriages. I was soon asleep once again, and did not wake up until the train stopped at Perth. Our next stop was Edinburgh, and I always got off there whenever possible. Then from a shop in Princes Street, I would purchase some Balkan Subrane, a wonderful smoke that I found even non-smokers enjoyed.

In a matter of minutes I was back on the train once again, and we were soon on the move. My next stop was Leicester, and following my Movement Order instructions, I soon reached my destination, the Military College of Science. There, once I had established my identity etc., I was told that I was in a particular class that began at eight the following morning, and directed to the room where I would sleep and stack my kit. It was all very regimental and well organised.

The following morning, I was on parade at 8am and surprised to see the number of Sergeants there. Everyone except the one in charge was either a Sergeant, Staff Sergeant or Warrant Officer Class II. We were marched away to our various classes where we were faced with a very large number of different field guns that I had never seen before. The instruction was good as the instructors were for the most part regular soldiers and knew their job well.

We took notes, and were examined each day on the lectures and demonstrations we had been given. I managed to struggle through, but at times was quite worried about the amount of technical information that I had to learn and retain.

In March, 1942, I was promoted to the rank of Staff Sergeant in the Royal Army Ordnance Corps, and the lessons went on. It was quite an unusual existence. We had to provide a guard at night, and this surprised many of us. Even more surprising was the fact that the night guard consisted of a Warrant Officer Class II and ten Staff Sergeants. It was a chore that we all had to take in our turn.

There were times when I felt my head would explode. There was so much to absorb and remember. We had been told when we arrived at the college that this was a course which in peacetime took four years to complete, and carried the rank of Staff Sergeant in the R.A.O.C.

We were taken through the whole operation of guns from the 3.7-inch Howitzer to the 5.5-inch Gun Howitzer almost to the last nut and bolt. Apart from the guns, we also had to learn how to strip, repair, assemble and maintain binoculars, compasses, telescopes, rangefinders and a number of other pieces of military hardware and accessories.

The day came in June, 1942, when the course ended and we were each told to report to the Regimental Office individually. None to my knowledge failed the course, although quite a number dropped out along the way.

I don't think any of us were cocky enough to say that we felt happy that we had passed until we were told by the Major in charge. He shook my hand, congratulated me and told me that I was now a Staff Sergeant Armament Artificer (Field), of the Royal Army Ordnance Corps. He handed me a Movement Order to report to the Second Infantry Brigade Workshops R.A.O.C. of the 1st Infantry Division, at East Dereham in Norfolk.

The 2ND Infantry Brigade Workshops

At East Dereham, I was welcomed by the Artificer Sergeant Major and taken to see the Commanding Officer, Major Dickie. I was told that I would be in charge of the Armament Section of the workshop, and taken around the part of the workshop that was to be my responsibility.

It was soon obvious that I had a lot more to learn. Apart from the normal hammer, chisel and file work of the fitters, there was turning, welding, blacksmithing and other artisan skills I would have to learn something about - without showing my ignorance of them. The opportunity to learn was there, and I was going to make damned sure that I learned my way round those subjects, new as they were to me.

I had now joined a very different outfit from the one that I had left behind in Orkney. Physical fitness was the order of the day. Five-mile runs, route marches and swimming in full kit formed part of a normal day's work. Everybody had to be able to swim, and I began to wonder just what I had got myself into.

Our blacksmith was a true master of his craft, but could not swim. He had been told that unless he could swim a length of the baths in full kit, he would be posted elsewhere. What an opportunity for a man who wanted to secure a safe posting in wartime! He desperately wanted to remain with his unit, and his friends and I wanted to retain him. He had taken the time to impart some of his vast knowledge to me, and I felt that I owed him something of a debt of honour. I spent quite some time with our blacksmith at the East Dereham swimming baths, and he finally managed to pass the test.

At East Dereham, I was promoted to Artificer Quartermaster Sergeant, Warrant Officer Class II, with the pay that went with it. I was now earning far more than I could ever earn in the Co-operative Wholesale Society, and probably more than a Police Constable.

It was at about this time that the Royal Electrical and Mechanical Engineers came into existence. The Royal Army Ordnance Corps became a Field Park, gathering in and looking after stores, while the engineering side of Ordnance Corps work was incorporated into R.E.M.E. Additionally, engineers were being drawn into the new military organisation from other regiments, producing a unit that carried out every type of engineering. I now became a member of R.E.M.E. Times were certainly changing in the army.

The amount of work that came into the workshop really surprised me. Rivets in the trail of some of the Brigade guns, twenty-five pounders, were loose. Some we would replace, others we were able to tighten up. The guns had only been fired a few times in training, after probably being in store for a long while. At least that seemed to be the obvious conclusion. The recuperator systems told the same story; many were either low in oil or leaking. This meant that many had to be stripped down and repacked.

The first one that I attacked made me think very hard. As I was the comparatively new boy put in charge of the Armament Section, many of my staff who were not sure of my ability paid particular attention to what I was doing. To the surprise of many, I encouraged this. I was determined to do the work myself, and demonstrate to them what had to be done, so that they in turn could do the job themselves without assistance when the time came.

I had only seen the inside of a recuperator when I was at the Military College of Science. Everything else I knew about. The working of the equipment, was from reading the handbooks on the guns. Thus, although determined to do the right thing and not let myself down in front of my men, I was obliged to take my time. To aid my bit of time-wasting, I gave a commentary on what I was actually doing at the time. The commentary did the trick; I could also see from the few odd questions which the demonstration prompted that they were happy with my work.

Late in 1942, the workshop moved to Kilmarnock in Scotland. We were located in Loanhead School, with the actual workshop being set up in the premises of the Scottish Motor Traction Company nearby. There was no indication as to where we were going from Kilmarnock, but the work we began doing left no doubt in our minds about the object of the next move. We were going on an invasion somewhere, that was for sure, though we had no idea where. One does not usually waterproof the engines of vehicles and extend the exhaust pipes over the driver's cab in normal circumstances.

Some thought that Norway was the most likely destination for our next posting, but it was unlikely that we would be going to Europe just yet. However, everyone was positive that it would not be the Middle East, because Montgomery was doing well out there. How very wrong the rumour-mongers could be!

It was about this time that I realised the irritation I had felt in my hands and face over the past couple of months was a little more serious than just a simple rash. I reported sick. The Medical Officer took one look at my hands and the right side of my face, and said, 'Bloody Hell, buffer oil poisoning.' I told him that I had never heard of that. His reply pointed out the logic of his statement. 'I've seen you chaps up to your elbows in buffer oil, doing re-packing work on the guns. I know that for once your hands end up looking very clean - apparently! But that's not the end of it, and hands can end up like yours have now. I've seen it all before.'

While he was saying all this, he was writing a short note on some official-looking notepaper. This he placed in an envelope and sealed it. On the envelope he had written: 'The Dermatologist, Royal Herbert Hospital, Woolwich.' He then told me to take it to the Orderly Room and they would give me a Movement Order to go to Woolwich, where they would be able to effect a cure.

You will appreciate that with all my thoughts more or less concentrated on the fact that we were obviously on the move, I was more than a little worried: worried about missing out on my new job, and being posted away from the 2nd. Infantry Brigade Workshops. I mentioned this to the M.O. and his reply took my worries away. 'Don't worry,' he said, 'they'll clear this up in about a week, especially when they know what caused the rash. They may paint you a few funny colours, but they've had plenty of these rashes to deal with, and know their job well.'

I was very relieved, and did as directed. That evening, I was on my way south to Woolwich and the Royal Herbert Hospital. When I reported there and was directed to the ward, I wondered whether I would find myself confronted by the battleaxe of a nurse who would have had me in the Guard Room on my earlier visits. I was, however, well received and looked after. Having cleaned my hands and the right side of my face, the nurse produced a bowl of modern woad.

I asked the nurse whether this was the concoction that our forefathers used to put on their faces to scare off invaders. She laughed, and was pleased to inform me that this was quite a modern mixture, called gentian violet, that was used on conditions like mine. Still with a chuckle in her voice, she told me not to worry, because they would have me out in about a week, although it would take a little longer to get it away from my face and hands.

Having telephoned home that day, I was very pleased, the following day, to have a visit from my father and a colleague of his, one Bill Chapman. Dad laughed at my condition, saying that I looked more like a clown than a soldier. Both of them, however, assured me that this violet stuff was recognised as the right thing to use on skin conditions. Their reassurance was most heart-warming, and I must say that by the time they had gone, the irritation was dying down.

My progress was good, and in just over a week I was on my way back to Kilmarnock. My hands and face, however, did not look entirely clean; in fact, I looked as if I had a bad case of' 'stubble trouble'! But I did at least have a clean bill of health, and was very pleased with the treatment I had received. The Royal Herbert Hospital was quite a hospital, and the staff certainly went out of their way to look after everyone.

Back in the workshop, I received a grand welcome home. There was still plenty of work being done, and the general consensus was that we would be on the move soon, 'any minute now'. In the Sergeants' Mess, we spent a lot of time disposing of our excess liquid stock, and a good time was had by all.

PART THREE

Overseas To North Africa

In the early hours of 26th January, 1943, we boarded our vehicles, tired and worn-out. We had worked through the previous day and far into the night, loading our vehicles, checking our equipment and organising the transportation of everything we felt we needed. We were off somewhere, but just where, we had no idea. The secret, thankfully, was well kept. It niggled us a little, but certainly did not worry us.

Secretly we were all pleased that the news of our move and destination had not been publicised throughout the unit. Our recent activity in the workshop was all the indication we needed. We were undoubtedly going to invade some foreign shore from the sea, and if the specific location was being kept secret from everyone, *really* everyone, there was less chance of us all entering a watery grave - a fate that had claimed many during this war.

Our shipping at this particular time was receiving some very unwelcome attention from Hitler's U-Boat packs and aircraft. Everyone in the unit could swim a length of the swimming baths in kit, enough, we felt, to get us to the nearest raft or something that would keep us afloat. We had gone through some very tough training in preparation for this, to get us into peak condition, and make us aware of what we might be faced with.

It is a very strange feeling, travelling in a military vehicle in your own country during war, knowing that you are going somewhere abroad. You know you are going to travel by sea, but have no idea just where you will land. To a man, we wanted to know where our destination was, but at the same time, we were relieved by the absence of such information. If we did not know, then we felt that 'Gerry' did not know either. I think we all settled for Norway, and just wanted to get on with the journey as soon as possible.

It seemed that we had hardly got ourselves comfortable (if that is the correct word to use for the transportation of troops in military vehicles) when our convoy came to a halt. We were at Gourock in the estuary of the River Clyde, and by 10am, we were all on board the S.S. Dunutter Castle. Here the men were ushered down into the bowels of the ship, where the holds had been modified to take rows of hammocks.

When I saw how cramped our living conditions would be, I very sincerely hoped that our journey would be short, very short indeed. This seemed to confirm our original idea that we were off to Norway: no fighting unit could live in such cramped conditions for very long, and return fighting fit to the outside world. I had a lot to learn.

Having got my men settled in, I began to wonder just what type of accommodation I would have. I certainly did not fancy hanging like a bat from a hammock in the hold! To my complete surprise, and great relief, I was directed to a second class cabin containing a proper bed complete with a mattress, clean white sheets, hot and cold water and a steward to ensure my creature comforts. Furthermore, the food in our Sergeants' Mess was great, and the service excellent. It was all like a dream. I was going to enjoy this.

Not only was the food good, but drink in our Mess was cheap, duty free in fact. The Sergeants' Mess was extremely comfortable, and we had nothing to do except relax, play cards and drink. There was no pressure from the powers that be to do this and that, in fact we rarely saw them. It was quite unreal, for the army normally never fails to find something which is a complete waste of time for the troops to do under similar circumstances.

The ship's engines started and stopped periodically, giving the false impression that we were on the move or moving. However, after this had happened on a number of occasions, we ignored the sound.

At two o'clock in the morning of 2nd March, 1943, I was awakened by the noise of the engines. I wondered why I had woken up, because I am normally a very sound sleeper. Then I realised that the engine noise was entirely different, certainly quieter, but there was a new throbbing throughout the ship that prompted me to get out of bed. Through the porthole I could see that we were well out to sea, with no land in sight.

I returned to my bed, thinking to myself that we would no doubt be off the coast of Norway very soon. I rose in the morning to a new and almost exciting experience - a walk round the deck, taking deep breaths of truly fresh air. It had the salty taste and smell that makes sea air so wonderfully different. As I walked round, I found myself repeating to myself, 'It's not a bad life, let's hope we can get away with it'. In the distance, on the port side of the ship, I could see islands. I had no idea where we were, but was satisfied in my mind that they must be the Orkney Islands.

Over breakfast, we discussed where we might be going, and finally agreed between ourselves that the islands had to be those off the coast of Ireland. We also agreed to a man that this was a most peculiar way to go to Norway, so the probability of our going to Norway slipped into the background.

After breakfast, we were called to assemble for Boat Drill. Very interesting. It was also very worrying, but put over extremely well. This was one drill that everyone paid strict attention to. The very big question that this drill posed was: could the odd floats and boats we had seen really cater for the very large number of troops on board the S.S. Dunutter Castle? A further unhappy question was prompted by the very considerable attention that our ships were receiving from the German U-Boats and planes. The ship's Captain assured us that every possible precaution had been and was still being taken to prevent such a disaster.

The 3rd March, found me carrying out the duties of Orderly Officer, an important duty in these particular circumstances, and somewhat different from the duties I had carried out in a similar capacity on dry land. I went down to the bowels of the ship with the Orderly Sergeant to check over the comforts of the troops, and there I found things most disconcerting. They were packed like rats in a trap, and the odour was foul. I was one of the lucky ones. I had never been seasick in my life, but I knew that if I had had to exist in that hold, sleeping in a hammock, it would not have been very long before I disposed of my last meal in a most unceremonious manner.

I felt extremely sorry for my comrades in arms who, due to the fact that they were junior in service or rank to myself, were obliged to live in such conditions. At the same time, I was secure in the knowledge that the British soldier possesses the ability to adapt to almost any situation. To a man, I found that they were all quite happily resigned to the fact that the Captain of the ship knew his job. I also found that the feeling below deck was still that we were heading for Norway.

During the next few days, life ran very smoothly for us all. Each day, we found that the convoy had grown. An extra ship or two arrived each night. The North Star had been on our Starboard Beam for two nights. This had the rumour-mongers churning out more 'latrinographs', as we fondly used to call their assessments. They had cracked it: we were going to the United States to link up with the Yanks, then we'd turn and invade Europe. That one really did not make sense to me, but still they came, educated guesses, projections and more rumour.

It is strange how continuous rumours on unknown matters manage to disturb one's train of thought. The result was that that night in the Mess, I sampled a few more glasses of beer than I normally did; I was not alone. I actually decided to try out the old piano that stood in the Mess, though I was (and am) not much of a pianist, nor, quite obviously, were my comrades particularly musical. There is, however, nothing like a few beers to loosen up the vocal chords and inhibitions, especially in circumstances such as we then found ourselves.

During the night of 7th March, I developed a cold and got up to go to the porthole for a breath of fresh air. The air was decidedly warmer than I had previously noted. As I stood thinking about the warmth of the night, I saw the North Star. Could it be the North Star? I asked myself. Yes. There was the Plough, and the brilliant star that had guided navigators and many unusual people over the ages.

The only trouble with this discovery was that when I had last noted this astral guide, it had been on the other side of the ship. It was now on the port side, and we were therefore travelling in an easterly direction. I returned to my bed but had difficulty in getting to sleep, as I was trying to work out just where we were actually going. I had heard enough rumours. Many probable locations passed through my mind, and then almost as if I had been counting sheep, I fell into the arms of Morpheus.

On the morning of 8th March, 1943, the sea was decidedly choppy. Our convoy consisted of about twelve ships, troopships and obvious military troop carriers with a Royal Navy escort. We had passed Gibraltar, and the weather was magnificent. The rumour-mongers were soon at it again. New bets were placed. They did not need us in Egypt. The choices were open: the South of France, Malta, Algeria and Tunisia. Then, while we were chewing over the possibilities, it happened. Guns fired some distance away. It was our Naval escort: we were being attacked by German planes. Depth charges were dropped. Then, above all of the noise, there was a distant explosion, and a vessel about a half mile behind us went up in smoke.

Fortunately for us, the Navy did a good job, as always. There had been a concerted attack by German war planes and U-Boats.

The planes sheered off, and one of the U-Boats was sent to the bottom of the sea. We did not stop to pick up survivors, but continued on our way. This seemed terrible at the time to us all, for we could have been the unlucky ship.

Algiers

In the circumstances, when you stop and think about it, it would have been an act of outright stupidity to have stopped. We could have been sitting ducks for whatever other planes might have been in the area, and the probability of other submarines around could never be discounted. Bitter past experience had taught our Royal Naval friends the folly of stopping for survivors in this deadly war.

On Tuesday, 9th March, 1943, the S.S. Dunutter Castle docked in Algiers, with only one ship lost, thanks to the tireless efforts of the Royal Navy; without them that journey would have been truly disastrous. The North African landings had been successful, and thereafter, the Allied forces continued their advances despite stiff opposition from German fighters and bombers. As for the ground fighting, news was somewhat sparse, though it seemed to suggest that the German army was in retreat, news that I must say pleased us all.

The relief of actually being moored up to dry land was immense. After ten days on board a ship that was the target for enemy attack, the experience was one I shall never forget. There was no probability of rest, however. The moorings were hardly made fast before we were disembarked and marched off away from the port area. Marched off! The thought of it at the time really hurt. After spending ten days in comparative luxury and comfort, with little or no exercise, I was very soft indeed. It was worse for the men, whose trip had been far from comfortable in the hold of the Dunutter Castle. But we marched eight miles, and then settled down in some farm buildings. This time we slept on bare ground; no more soft beds and clean sheets for me!

Despite my aching bones and exhaustion, sleep did not come that night. The ground was hard, damned hard, and I just could not settle down. Then it was 6am and reveille. Breakfast at 6.30am, bully beef and biscuits with a mug of tea from a dixie; no more steward waking me up with a nice cup of freshly-brewed tea.

Then we were on the move again. More marching and a further eight miles. This time we were beginning to realise just how much the 'cruise' had softened us all up, despite the men's cramped conditions and our previous training. Quite a few of the lads were having difficulty during the march, and those of us who were fairly fit took some of their equipment from them to help them out. We had done plenty of marching prior to leaving Scotland, but certainly not loaded up in the manner that we now found ourselves. On top of all that, it was quite hot by British standards. We were therefore all praying that we would get to our destination, wherever it was, very soon.

Our prayers were answered in due time, and we settled down once more in some other farm buildings. We had arrived at the outskirts of a village called Maison Carré, but rest and sleep were not to be.

Many were reading lectures: survival training, coupled with instructions and advice on how to treat the Arabs in the vicinity, was the order of the day. Finally, we bedded down in a huge barn. I say bedded down, but collapsed was more like it. Here the only disturbance was visited upon us at night.

One time an army boot landed with a crash against the wall of the barn near me, waking me suddenly. I heard a commotion over the other side of the barn. One of the lads said he had been woken up by what he thought was the sniffing of a small dog. It turned out to be a very big rat. Being a good soldier, he was sleeping with his head on his boots. He therefore threw one at the rat. Others amongst us had not seen the animal, and initially decided that it was either the soldier's imagination, a bad dream, or he had partaken of too much of the local red wine.

But no. Our unwanted visitor turned out to be very real, the biggest rat that any of us had ever seen or heard of. It made regular forays into our midst to raid our kit, notwithstanding the fact that whoever was the first to be disturbed would throw the nearest item of kit, usually a boot, at the intruder. We nicknamed the rat 'The Snuffler', as it did indeed make a noise like a panting dog. Furthermore, regardless of the missiles that were thrown at it, the mischievous rodent would return sometimes three or four times during the night.

Our sojourn in Maison Carreé ended at 4am on Tuesday 16th March, 1943. A new experience awaited us. We marched to a railway siding and were loaded into cattle trucks. Each truck bore that well known marking - *'8 cheveaux, 40 hommes'* - with no mention of kit. We were told that we were en route to Bone, which would be our next stop. Quite a journey, and we were wondering about our creature comforts, for the journey would take two to four days - depending.

Bone

Depending on what? we asked. It depends on whether the Luftwaffe decide to alter the layout of the railway lines to Bone, we were told. Needless to say, there were no toilets on this type of train. Thankfully, we went on our way with only this one minor worry; the train driver had thought of everything. The train would stop every now and then to enable the occupants to answer the calls of nature. Then there would be a whistle or toot from the train, and it would start to move off. We would then have to run back and climb aboard, many still holding up their trousers as they were helped back on to the cattle truck.

The journey, thankfully, was not interrupted by the Luftwaffe, and we arrived in Bone at 6.30am on 19th March, 1943. Here we camped beside the sea. Not a bad location. The weather was warm, and the sea looked good. After being cooped up in those cattle trucks, my first desire was to jump in for a swim in that lovely warm and inviting water.

The opportunity did not present itself until later in the day. Then, donning my navy blue army P.T. shorts, I ran down the beach and dived into the sea. The shock was intense. The water was cold, damned cold, and I came out a lot quicker than I had gone in. I was not the only one to find the water cold. The consensus of those who were supposed to know was that the Mediterranean is a deep sea, therefore retains its chill.

We now had a further journey ahead of us, again in cattle trucks. This time our destination was to be Teboursouk. We had grown accustomed to this unusual form of travel on our journey from Maison Carreé, and hoped that although we would be getting nearer to where the fighting was, we would have a peaceful trip. I think it was the next day when we stopped at Bou Salem.

Teboursouk

There, waiting for us, were some of our workshop vehicles, and also some Royal Army Service Corps transport. We boarded these, and were taken to a farm in Teboursouk, where we set up our workshop in the farm outbuildings. We could hear the sound of gunfire in the distance, and tried to assess just how far away the fighting was. Distant it may have seemed, but in fact it was not all that far away. We very soon found ourselves heavily engaged in repairing guns and equipment damaged in the fighting, which was only a few miles away.

The North African landing had been very successful, and for this we were grateful. The First Army that we were part of was able to continue its advances despite the stiff opposition put up by the German troops. At Teboursouk we worked very hard. One of the tasks I found myself involved in quite regularly was removing over-gauged rounds from guns. This was not a subject that had been covered in our lectures at either Woolwich or at the Military College of Science. The first one I had in was a twenty-five-pounder gun.

The tool used for this purpose is known as the ejector projectile. It is a large heavy brass implement, and a most useful tool. It is turned so that it just fits into the barrel of the gun, and is bored so that one end fits over the nose cone of the projectile. For handling, it has a stout pole fitted into the other end.

Over-gauged rounds are generally those that have an extra thick driving band. What gun crews are expected to do in the line is to elevate the gun slightly, and place the ejector projectile down the barrel, and ram down on the projectile with it. Normally, the round comes out fairly quickly and is caught at the breech by one of the gunners. The trouble arises when the actual girth of the round is oversized, and jams in the barrel. With the first one I tried the normal method, as had the gunners, but I could not move the projectile. I decided to remove the stout pole fitted, and obtained a piece of round timber that fitted the barrel, first lowering the brass cup ejector on its own, then the larger pole. I tried with a fourteen-pound hammer, but was unable to shift the offending projectile. I had to think of something else.

I hooked the gun to the front of the heavy Scammel recovery lorry and drove it, pushing the gun forward sharply into the trunk of a large nearby tree. After four attempts I managed to free the round.

On arrival back at the workshop, I found that none of my men was there. Looking round I saw a young officer who had apparently come in with the gun crew walking towards me waving his hand. I got down and asked him what he wanted. He started in a most excited manner by calling me all the fools in Christendom and telling me that I was lucky not to have blown up myself, the Scammel and the gun.

I finally managed to stop his abuse, and asked where my men were. 'I told them to get away from here,' he said. I gave this young man a lecture on the workings of fusing ammunition, explaining that none of it is normally in exploding mode until it has actually been fired, and that it is only the centrifugal force that makes the small shutters clear from the arming mechanism.

I don't think even then that this young man took in any of what I had said; he was too intent on giving me trouble. I finally said to him, 'I have nothing further to say to you. If you want to continue insulting me, go and see my commanding officer.' With that, I saluted, turned and walked away.

My men were enjoying a break over tea in the cookhouse, and I told them to finish their tea and return to the workshop. As I left the cookhouse, Captain Troup came in and walked over to me. 'What have you done to that young Artillery Officer?' he said. I told him what had happened, and he laughed and walked away.

Shortly after that Major Dickie came into the workshop on one of his unannounced visits. 'Mr Swain, I hope you knew what you were doing just now. You scared that young Artillery Officer,' he said. I apologised for scaring the man, but said that I had only been doing what I had done successfully a number of times before. Also, I mentioned that if the officer wanted to talk down to people, he should make sure he knew what he was talking about. He then asked me where my staff were. I told him that the Artillery Officer had sent them away and that they were having a break on his instructions, but would be back soon.

The Major stiffened, his eyes flashed and he said, 'Did he?' before striding away, probably to look for the young officer. I have no idea what happened after that. What I do know is that I successfully removed many obstinate rounds from various guns in the same fashion, in various places during the war - without mishap, as you will appreciate.

During the recent interruption I had noticed a young Arab lad apparently working in the cookhouse area. I went to the Sergeant cook, and asked what he was doing there. 'Oh,' he said, 'you mean Dropta? A bloody good worker that one, he does any job I give him, and he doesn't ask for any pay.' I pointed out that I had not heard of that name before, although the slang connotation was rather obvious. The Sergeant laughed 'He'll do any dirty job I give him, and has even volunteered to dig latrines.' At the time I could see Dropta working away at something over one of the stoves.

I walked over to see just what he was doing. There was a sheet of metal about a quarter of an inch thick and roughly two feet square, over the flames of the stove. On the metal was a heap of damp tea-leaves. He was stirring these with a piece of rusty metal, and on the ground beside him was a large dixie with the leaves still in it. I asked him what he was doing. He seemed a little worried and fumbled in his gallabeer. Producing what looked like an old cocoa tin and opening it, he poured some of the contents on to the sheet of metal. He then scooped them up again. The contents looked like tea-leaves ready for use.

The Sergeant cook broke in to tell me that all Dropta asked for as payment for his work was to have the tea-leaves from the tea dixies. He would dry them out and sell the dried leaves to his neighbours. It seemed that in a misguided moment, when he was doing the same work for another regiment, he had sold some of the fried-up tea-leaves to some of his own people. They beat him up. He ran back to the army camp and told the cook what had happened. The cook told him that he had dropped a clanger and named him 'Dropta'.

He was very proud of that name, and had even mentioned it to his people. They liked the name, and encouraged him to carry on with this type of work, as long as he did not try to sell the results of his labours in his own village. Such enterprise had to be appreciated, and I found it difficult to suppress a chuckle, at the same time feeling sorry for anyone who tried to make a proper cup of tea from his efforts.

We broke camp about a month after the incident with the young Artillery Officer, and moved along behind the battle that was fast nearing its end. Our first stop was at Testour, a few miles southwest of Medjes El Bab. Here we remained in an olive grove for about a fortnight. We had a few short moves after that, stopping overnight at various locations. Then we came to a halt by a prisoner of war camp near Hammam Lif. Here it was that I was struck down with a spot of gut trouble, and sent to the field hospital with suspected dysentery on 25th May. This was after I had made trips to Infidaville and Monastir. Thankfully, it was not dysentery, just a spot of diarrhoea, and after treatment I was released on Friday 28th May, 1943.

Sousse

I went to Infidaville the following day, but did not sample any of the local food as I had before. One case of diarrhoea was enough, even though the food tasted very pleasant. On my return to camp, I found to my surprise that there were four seventeen-pounder guns in for my examination and report. Very interesting guns, with a field gun and anti-tank gun facility that was most impressive.

After attending to these guns, on my return to camp, we were on the move again. Sousse was to be our next location. This was an interesting posting, for here there were plenty of bombed-out buildings where I could get much needed metal for repair work. We went out on the scrounge on a number of occasions, and our target was more often than not channel iron or angle iron, which we found in plenty. Something was afoot, but what? There was no apparent reason or immediate use for the seventeen-pounders. Neither, for that matter, was there any apparent good or urgent reason for suddenly having to manufacture and weld on spare wheel carriers for the Humber Medium armoured cars.

We were kept extremely busy in the workshop, where even the rumour-mongers could not suggest where our next move would be. With so much destruction behind us and before our eyes in the city of Sousse, it was good to receive an opportunity on 9th June to visit the holy city of Kairouan. A leave truck was allocated, and I have to say that this city is one that was well and truly worth the visit.

From Sousse, we also had the opportunity to visit Tunis on occasions, and the trips were always welcome. I had developed a liking for cigars in my travels, and in Tunis one could purchase a bundle of twenty cigars for the equivalent of about two pounds in francs. They went down well, and were enjoyed by all.

There was a lot of movement of stores within the workshop, which indicated that we were on the move again, but with no clue as to where or how far. There was call for more metal, and I spent a lot of time with an oxy-acetylene cutter, gathering up metal for further repairs.

Kelibia

Late in June, we moved from Sousse to Kelibia at the tip of Cap Bon. Here we set up workshop in what was the old Custom House, and we set about repairing some of the very heavily damaged and worn-out weapons and vehicles that were still with the Division. The rumour-mongers were soon at it again We were going to leave North Africa, and would be going to France, Italy or one of the islands in the Mediterranean. This was without doubt the lull before the storm.

The army is very good at doing as much as possible to ensure that the troops get in as much rest, relaxation and leave, call it what you may, before moving onwards. Here at Cap Bon, despite the fact that we had so much work to get on with, we were, to our surprise, permitted some very delightful periods of rest and leave. In fact, each day, a lorry left camp at 9am with twenty or thirty men, heading for Tunis. It would return shortly after 10pm. I was fortunate enough to manage this trip on one or two occasions, and very welcome indeed they were.

Tunis is a very interesting place, and I enjoyed exercising my scant knowledge of French on the inhabitants. On one such occasion, I met a husband and wife named Gonthier, who lived at Saint Germain, a village just outside Tunis, which we passed on our way in. They invited me to visit them on my next trip to Tunis, and I gladly accepted.

Thus it was that on my next trip to Tunis, I got the driver to drop me off at Saint Germain. I told him to pick me up at the same place at 8.40 that night on his way back to camp. The day went well, and I had a meal of French cooking that was truly wonderful, followed by a lot of talking in French which we all enjoyed. I was picked up on time, and returned to camp very pleased at having spent an interesting day with a French family.

Living in a makeshift hut on the beach by the workshop at Kelibia was a Spaniard named Batiste. He was a fisherman, and apparently made his living catching crabs, octopus and various fish from the area. During those warm evenings, Batiste would cook his own food by his hut on the beach and was never more pleased than when I or one or two soldiers who could speak a little French came to sit and talk with him. Sometimes he produced the wine, sometimes we did. He could speak no English, but he was a very interesting person.

Our friendship grew to the extent that he would bring fish to the Sergeants' Mess, and would not take a cent from us. All went well until some of the lads in a light-hearted and unthinking manner 'borrowed' his rowing boat. They got into difficulties in the treacherous seas of the areas, and were thought to be truly lost at sea. Batiste was hopping mad at the loss of his boat, and despite our many efforts to assure him that we would put matters right for him, we were unable to console him in any way.

We even promised to find Batiste another boat, but to no avail. The following day, Bob Phillips, a Sergeant in the Divisional Field Security Police, who I knew well, turned up at the camp. The visit was no accident; it was connected with the disappearance of Batiste's rowing boat. We all wondered why the Field Security Police was taking an interest, and not the Military Police of the Divisional Provost Company, which was normal if a theft had been reported.

Fortunately for all concerned, at about this time the soldiers who had 'borrowed' the rowing boat for their joy ride came ashore at Menzel Temime, about ten miles south of our camp. The troops were given severe warnings about tampering with any property belonging to others. The peculiar point was that, despite King's Regulations, there was no indication that the offenders would be charged or disciplined. Everyone wondered what was behind such a decision.

Here at Kelibia, there was a stone jetty that extended into about five feet of water. It was ideal for a shallow dive. There was also the obvious result of an exploded bomb in the sea about twenty-five yards offshore. This was ideal for swimming and fishing. I had never been able to see underwater, so I fished using an old Italian gas mask. With the pipe extended to the side of my head and just out of the water when my head was breaking the surface, it was perfect. In my right hand I held a tank antennae to which was attached a length of thread. At the end of this I put a homemade hook fashioned out of a sewing needle. For bait, I used shrimps. In the centre of the bomb hole the troops had put an old fifty-gallon oil drum which was filled with rocks. It was just meant for diving from, but I used to stand on it and fish occasionally.

All went well until one day in July. I was making my way back to the oil drum with a fish in my hand when I felt a bump in the middle of my back. Batiste, who was watching me from the shore, shouted and signalled for me to come ashore quickly.

According to Batiste, I had scratched my back, probably on the oil drum, and a young barracuda had taken a nip at me. Closer examination revealed that I had obviously grazed my back by leaning against the oil drum, and had bled very slightly. Batiste insisted that I was very fortunate that it was only a very small barracuda. This 'tiddler' had taken a piece of flesh from my back about a half inch across. Had it been its father, the bite would have been a lot bigger. We were all very grateful for this information. We continued swimming in the bomb hole after this, but it was generally cleared first with the aid of a hand grenade.

There were clearly moves afoot in the Division. This was not advertised, but we knew from the movement of troops and equipment that something was going to happen somewhere. Shortly after the barracuda incident, there were raids on the islands of Lampadusa, and Pantalaria, which men from the Division took part in. These raids were apparently most satisfactorily carried out without heavy losses, and the islands were secured.

I was to learn later that the success of this operation was largely as the result of information and assistance provided by Batiste. He knew the islands and the sea of the area well. So well, in fact, that he had even rowed his small boat over to those islands during the course of some of his fishing expeditions.

Early in the morning of 13th August, 1943, Batiste came to me and wanted me to go out in his boat with him. He asked me to bring a grenade with me. 'Just one,' he said, 'I can get enough fish for all of you if you bring a grenade.' I believed him; I had seen the result of a grenade when I had used one on the bomb hole.

Batiste rowed his boat round the headland to a small inlet into the rocks about fifty yards long. Slowly he rowed into the inlet, and finally stopped and peered over the side of the boat. He laid a small piece of wood on the water and rowed on.

At about thirty feet from the piece of wood, he signalled for me to throw the grenade to the piece of wood. This I did. As the grenade exploded below the surface, Batiste dived into the sea. He came up with two large fish threaded on to the fingers of each hand, with one in his mouth. These he threw on to the boat, and went down again, and again, pitching his catch on to the boat each time he surfaced.

This was a new style of fishing to me, but the end result was appreciated by the men all round. It was Batiste's swimming that amazed me. He seemed to be able to remain underwater for such a long time while he collected the stunned fish. It was from Bob

Phillips, who I told the story to, that I learned that Batiste had attended (quite of his own accord) the scene of a British naval vessel that had been sunk by the Germans off Cap Bon. Batiste had dived into the sea and rescued a great many British sailors. He had finally collapsed from exhaustion, and was treated by the naval surgeon present, who expressed great admiration for his work.

Hammamet

Within a few days of the fishing incident with the grenade, the workshop moved on to new location in an olive grove close to the sea at Hammamet. A wonderful location. It was here that I was suddenly overcome by a slight form of blindness. I knew what it was, and cursed myself silently. I had been involved in a lot of electric welding of more spare wheel brackets on the back of Humber Medium armoured cars for the Division. I had not been as careful as I should have been. In fact, I was the victim of that old saying, 'Familiarity breeds contempt.' I had been careless in bringing up the visor before I struck the arc.

I was taken off to the nearby field hospital, where a wise Medical Officer introduced me to a brown concoction that I still attempt to obtain whenever possible: 10% Argyrol. When he put the first drops into my eyes, it was as if I was wearing sunglasses, and the stuff ran down my face. Catching some of the drops in my handkerchief, I saw it looked like iodine, but this was what was giving the sunglasses effect, and sensation of relief.

I managed to get hold of a pair of decent sunglasses with side protection, and took things a little easy after this scare, leaving more of the work to others. Bill Croft and Stan Westall, our two welders, were masters of their craft, and I had only joined in the welding when one of them had been hospitalised with stomach trouble.

I took a walk in to Nabeul, and had a pleasant time even though I found wearing sunglasses at night difficult. I was, however, slowly getting used to them, and thankfully my eyes were not hurting as they had been. It was the change in the strength of the light that affected me more than anything. The lights in a cafe, after I'd been in the darkened roadways, immediately made my eyes run again.

It was on about 24th August, 1943, that I decided to take the leave truck to Tunis and get the driver to drop me off at Saint Germain once again. As I left the truck, I told the driver to pick me up at the same place at eight o'clock that evening.

I found the Gonthiers' house, and was once again greeted with open arms. They were delighted to see me after such a long while. There followed a long chat about the war and life in general, and they complimented me on my improved French. We finally went up on to the roof of their house, where a truly wonderful meal was produced. Madam Gonthier set it out as if it was a Lord Mayor's banquet, and I could not have asked for more: superb food, plenty of wine, and excellent company.

At seven thirty that evening, I bid my friends goodbye and left, promising to return when next passing. I waited as arranged at the selected spot for the leave truck to arrive. By nine-thirty, it had not appeared, and my heart sank. How I was going to get out of this one was the thought foremost in my mind. I returned to the Gonthiers' house, explained what had happened, and asked if I could sleep on their roof for a few hours. No problem, I was told. Madam Gonthier put up a camp bed for me on the roof. I told her that at first light I would depart, and attempt to get back to my unit before I was declared absent without leave.

I slept very little that night, and was up at dawn. Then, silently bidding farewell to my friends, I left. I was fit and walking did not worry me. Then I began to think. I had to cover about sixty miles to Hammamet. As I kept walking, British vehicles passed me by, but we were not hitchhike-minded like the Americans. After some seven or eight miles, an American truck pulled up for me. I got in, and was later dropped off at a fork in the road near Hammam Lif. My American 'knight' continued towards Grombalia, while I was obliged to take a comparatively minor road toward Menzel-Bou-Zelfa, in the direction of Nabeul.

After yet another few miles, I was picked up by another American truck. I was not doing badly. The last ten miles, however, was a march I shall never forget. Having eaten and drunk well the previous day, and slept very little, I was tired, damned tired. I was, in fact, mentally and physically nearly exhausted.

Apart from all that, and no doubt adding to my mental fatigue, was the big worry about the reception I would receive on my arrival back at camp. As I approached within a mile of the camp, I was turning over in my mind just what to say to Major Dickie, my Commanding Officer. The Major did not like me very much, in fact I don't think he liked anyone below his station in life. He was a lifetime engineer, and had doubts about anyone who was not also a lifetime engineer. Furthermore, he had demonstrated that he knew his job from A to Z.

Thankfully, if you could do your job, he left you alone. If you could not do your work to his complete satisfaction, you did not last long in his unit. He gave me little trouble, but I was always aware that he kept a very close eye on me. He had been known to refer to wartime soldiers like myself, who had learned their engineering skills in the army, as 'ten-week wonders'. He also had a most critical manner when talking to those under him, a manner that made the back hairs of my neck stand on end. He could be so irritating.

My mind was in turmoil. Should I just creep into my tent and make out that I had overslept? How I would have loved to do just that, but I had not given it much thought. Major Dickie may have been a strange man, but he was not a man to lie to, and I had neither the guts or inclination to lie to him.

As I walked past the sentry, the Guard Commander acknowledged me. I nodded back to him and kept walking. The Major had a fifteen hundredweight truck which he kept as a mobile office. He was sitting at his desk writing, apparently deeply engrossed in whatever he was doing. I marched up to the truck, halted, stood smartly to attention, saluted and in a loud voice said, 'A.Q.M.S. Swain reporting from absence, Sir.' He lifted his head and looked at me as if I was something the cat had brought in. He said nothing for what seemed an age. As for me, I just stood stiffly to attention, not a little scared, and not knowing what his next move would be.

Probably only a minute went by, but it was definitely the longest minute I had ever experienced. Then he spoke; slowly, deliberately and forcefully, with me concentrating on his every word. 'Don't play games with me, Mr Swain. Get about your work, and I'll see you later.' There was an unspoken element of malice in his words. He was quite obviously making up his mind as to the best method of dealing with me to my least advantage. Furthermore, he seemed to be enjoying every minute of my suspense. I said nothing, just saluted, turned and went to my tent.

I had a good clean up, deep in thought. I had a very distinct feeling that I had volunteered for whatever was going to happen next. I was satisfied in my mind that I had not been missed by Major Dickie, so decided to just get on with my work and wait. Later that morning, I was stripped to the waist repacking the recuperator system of a twenty-fiive-pounder gun when the Major came round. He stopped by me and smiled. That worried me; he had never done it before.

'How are you getting on, Mr Swain?' he asked.

'All right, Sir,' I replied.

'Did you have a good time yesterday, Mr Swain?' he asked.

Here it comes, I thought to myself. He was still smiling, and that was the worry. 'Yes, Sir,' I replied.

'Very interesting,' he said. Then the smile went from his face, and the hard, analytical look that I knew so well returned. 'The next time you have a very interesting time on leave, Mr Swain, I will dispose of you as I would dispose of an old coat.' He turned as he pronounced the last words, and thankfully walked off. I heard nothing more about the incident.

My knowledge of French continued to stand me in good stead, but I was always careful after the Saint Germain incident to return to camp on time. My continued vigilance, however, nearly came to an end shortly afterwards when I went on a trip to Tunis with the leave truck, just for a rest from the work that seemed to be ever increasing.

Meeting The French Foreign Legion

In an Arab café in Tunis, I got into conversation with some French Foreign Legion lads. They were a truly mixed bag, and their Sergeant Major and I got along like the proverbial house on fire, in a mixture of French and Arabic. Everything was going well until the arrival of some American soldiers.

Upon entering the cafe, they took exception to the fact that a group of soldiers were speaking to the café proprietor in Arabic. A fight started, and some more American soldiers arrived. I personally never look for a fight, but I had to support my new-found friends, for the Americans were half drunk and well out of order.

The disagreement became quite a dust-up and we were giving a very good account of ourselves. The flimsy tables and chairs took the brunt of the punishment, with the very frightened proprietor attempting to safeguard his stock behind the bar. Suddenly there was a shout of 'Snowdrops!'

The fighting stopped and the Americans ran out of the café straight into the arms of their Military Police. Frankly I felt no pity for them, for they had started this shindig and had asked for whatever they got, either from us or their 'Snowdrops'.

I found myself being guided through the rear of the premises by the proprietor and two Frenchmen. We made our way from the café area as quickly as possible. Then, as if by some pre-arranged plan, we - that is, the French Foreign Legion group - all met up in another Arab café about a half mile from the scene of the previous incident. I was apparently their hero; they had decided this on the grounds that I had stood beside them in the fight against the Americans. I went to a lot of trouble to explain to them that the Americans were our allies and comrades in arms and so, for that matter, were the French troops. My reason for standing with them was quite simply that I had been with them when the Americans started the fight. Had it been British soldiers who had started the fight, I would still have stood with them.

My Foreign Legion friends seemed to have some difficulty in understanding my brand of British logic. Then, to assist them in their deliberations, one of the number produced a bottle of *zibibb*. I had never tasted this very pleasant drink before. It was not sharp like whisky or sweet like gin. It was very pleasant indeed. I began to enjoy the taste, and the company.

I was nevertheless somewhat frightened of missing the leave truck back to camp, and told them I must leave. That, they said, was OK by them, but I would have to have another, for the *Entente Cordiale*. Then another, and another. 'Don't worry about your leave truck,' I was told. 'We are stationed in Nabeul, and will take you back to your camp.' I felt a little more at ease. Perhaps it was the company, perhaps it was the demon *zibbib* taking effect. Maybe it was relief that my lift back to camp was assured. Or maybe I was just past caring.

My French friends took me back to camp at Hammamet in their truck, and although I do not remember much of the journey, I arrived back in good time. I may have been feeling a little merry, but was certainly not drunk or anywhere near. I made my way to my tent quietly and slept very soundly indeed.

The following morning, I was awake early as usual. I washed in my canvas bucket as usual, and shaved with my cut-throat razor as usual. The Sergeants' Mess Orderly brought me my morning cup of tea, as usual. I loved that first morning cup of tea, and sat down to enjoy it. Now to work. I felt good.

I got up after finishing my tea. I definitely did not feel so good. Most unusual! Then, to my horror, I realised that I was rather drunk. Or perhaps I had eaten something that did not agree with me? I sat down to think this through.

Tiny Morris, the A.S.M., was nearby, carrying out his usual morning toilet, and I called him over. He just laughed. 'You had more than your fair share yesterday, John. You were bloody pickled.' I could not believe it. I had been quite clear-headed and steady when I got out of bed a few minutes earlier. Now I was anything but steady.

I was convinced that whatever ailed me just had to be one of those strange and unaccountable illnesses that had struck down so many of the troops during our travels across North Africa: malaria, sand-flly fever, dysentery. These all passed through my mind, but none seemed to fit the bill. I sent for the Medical Orderly. He came in looking all serious and concerned. Then he too just laughed. For a moment I was annoyed and nearly said something stupid. Then, just as I was going to tell him a few home truths, he started talking. 'We shall call this suspected malaria,' he said. 'Stay in your bed, and above all don't drink anything. Nothing at all.' Quite a speech, I thought.

I rolled myself up in my blankets and tried to sleep. I felt ashamed, a fraud. My mouth felt as dry as a bone. I had to have a drink of something. But no, the Medical Orderly had been quite firm, and I knew that he knew his business. By midday, I was feeling a lot better and got up. I had not been missed by Major Dickie, and all was well. Our Medical Orderly, however, saw me leave the tent and was quick to pull me to one side. 'If you're daft enough to drink North African firewater, *zibbib*, or the likes, you must do

125

what you're told. The next drink of any sort that you take will make you as drunk as you were earlier in the day. You just have to take it easy for at least three days, and I'll tell you what and when you can drink.'

He was right, of course and so I was cautious. I laid up that day, and drank nothing despite my cracked throat. The members of the Mess were sympathetic, and said they hoped I did not have malaria. They tempted me with whisky, and could not understand why I would not partake with them.

The following morning, the medic came to see me again. 'You're doing well,' he said, 'but I have to be sure it's not malaria, or something like that. Another day's rest will do no harm. It was not until the third day that I was able to settle down to a normal routine and relax while enjoying my work; and I did truly enjoy my work. For the record, however, I have definitely left Pernod, *arraq* and *zibbib* alone since that fateful outing.

In late August, I decided to try out my little vest pocket camera which had been sent to me from home. What brought about this idea was the sight of a spot of Arab irrigation that must have dated back to Biblical days. It was about the nearest thing to perpetual motion that I had ever seen.

A very deep hole had been dug at one side of a field, and the earth piled up by the hole. This had been beaten down to a firm slope. At the top of the slope two stout poles had been driven in, and across the top of the two poles a third pole secured them together.

On the ramp was a camel. A rope secured to a harness on the camel had been passed over the third pole. The camel walked up the ramp, and the rope with a bullock skin sack-cum-bucket at the end was lowered down the hole. When the camel got to the top of the ramp, it turned and walked back down the ramp. When the bullock skin bucket hit the cross beam or pole, it tipped the water out of the skin. The water then ran down the ramp and was taken away in small narrow gullies that had been cut into the ground to wherever it was required. The camel was alone, and carried on like this all day, and perhaps through the night. I had occasionally seen an Arab near the ramp, but he did not stay long, and the camel seemed to know just what was required.

My men had noticed my interest in the camel at this watering hole. All of them were forever collecting souvenirs. The Germans, who had now left North Africa, had been known to dispose of their excess weaponry by throwing them into these wells. The watering hole was therefore a source of souvenirs that had not previously been tapped.

Searching With An Electric Magnet

With two of my fitters, I went over to this well when there was no sign of the camel. Peering down into the dark hole, I could see that it was between twenty and thirty feet deep. How deep the water was at the bottom was anyone's guess, but the way the bucket had been hoisting the water out suggested that it was very deep. The sides of the hole seemed to be just stones when it was down about six feet, the first six feet being just a form of top soil. Then one of the lads let out a shout. 'Look at that!' He was pointing to what looked like the magazine of an automatic pistol lodged in the stones, almost all of it showing.

There had to be pistols in this well, and pistols meant money. The Yanks would pay all sorts of prices for pistols, that was well known. We were not hard up, but a little extra cash for true souvenirs of Arab workmanship would go down well. Pulling out the guns, or whatever was down this well, should be no problem. I felt that if I could get hold of an electric magnet, perhaps I might find something useful.

Thereafter, I let it be known amongst the lads who brought their equipment in for repair that I wanted an electric magnet to assist me in my work. It would have been silly to let them know what I wanted it for, so I kept the reason quiet. Within a few days, I had my magnet. It worked on twenty-four volts, no problem. I linked up two twelve-volt batteries in series and it worked quite well. The next stage was to get it into the well. This was not easy. To our surprise, we found that the water at the bottom of the well was only about two or three feet deep. Furthermore, lowering the magnet over the side of the well was not a very good idea. It was too heavy to keep it away from the sides on the way down. We neither wanted to damage the magnet on the way down, nor knock off anything it had picked up on its way up. Then one of the lads had a bright idea. 'Lower me down, and I'll take the magnet with me.'

This sounded like a good idea. I located a Jeep, a good length of rope and an old tyre. I threw the rope over the cross beam at the top of the ramp, tied the tyre to the end of the rope and secured the other end of the rope to the Jeep-towing hook. Our volunteer decided to have a dummy run and sat in the tyre. Gently he was lowered down until he told us to stop. He then threw up the magazine that we had first seen. It was from a Luger pistol. When he came up we gave him the magazine.

Lowering him down once again was no trouble. He called for us to stop when he was about two feet from the water. He lowered the magnet into the water and asked to be pulled up. As he came up, I could see that he had a German rifle on the magnet. Unfortunately, as he tried to pull it out of the water, it fell off. We tried again and again. We did find some pieces of Luger and Mauser pistols, but not one complete pistol. There were all sorts of other metal objects down there.

George Croft, our volunteer, called up asking to be lowered nearer to the water, so that he could get hold of anything that the magnet picked up. He was duly lowered until his feet were almost touching the water. He found more small pieces of rifle and pistol, but could not get hold of any larger items before they dropped off. Then he let out a loud shout. 'Get me out of here! Snakes!' I signalled to the Jeep, and George was hoisted up to the top of the well in double quick time.

The sunburned George Croft was shaking. 'There are dozens of bloody snakes down there! If you want to go down there you're welcome, but not me.' That was enough for me too. We abandoned our quest for souvenirs, but it was quite an experience. The sum total of our excursion into the well was about five very rusty pistol and rifle magazines. The only item that was of any use was one side lock plate from a Luger pistol. We had found Lugers before, but never with the side lock plate in situ, and even with all of our fitting ability and equipment, it was virtually impossible to make a copy.

An Epitaph to 'Bull'

Normally we would not have been able to enjoy our attempts to find souvenirs, but under the current workshop circumstances things were different. We were usually far too busy, but at that time there was an unusually slack period, a lull. No-one knew why; all we knew was that General Eisenhower was up to something. Nobody, however, was even prepared to hazard a guess as to what this would be.

As if in answer to our inner questioning, we were all called on parade at two o'clock one afternoon. Then, with the exception of the camp guard, we were all marched out of the camp area to a large open space about half a mile away. Here we were given foot drill by Sergeant Doubtfire and A.S.M. Morris. It was most unusual, marching twenty abreast across a field, and attempting to keep abreast in straight line. We flogged away at this all afternoon in the heat, and finally managed to satisfy those in charge. This was a workshop, not used to continuous drills of this style.

Back in the Mess, I spoke to Tiny Morris. 'What the hell's going on?' I asked.

'Simple, John,' he replied. 'Our Commander-in-Chief, General Eisenhower, wants to have a look at the Division. Therefore, the First Infantry Division will be marched en masse in front of him early next month. He wants to either thank us for our efforts in North Africa, or tell us where we'll be going next. You'll have to wait and see, John.'

I don't know whether it was the heat of the marching or the welding in the workshop earlier that morning, but I had another spot of near blindness that evening. I moved off to the field hospital again, and got from them another bottle of 10% Argyrol. What a wonderful mixture that was, and it certainly helped me.

With the march past taking up every spare minute in drills, we now also spent a lot of time scrubbing equipment that had not received much attention for months, and polishing cap badges and belt buckles which all had to be laid out for Major Dickie and Ted Doubtfire to inspect.

It was my impression that Bill Morris, the turner, made a few shillings with his buff in the machinery lorry. Our aged equipment looked surprisingly shiny and clean when he had finished with it, and there were few complaints from Major Dickie. I was just thankful that we had no urgent work at the time.

The big parade was on 4th September, 1943, and all we left behind at camp was a fire picket and the guard. For once there had been a queue clamouring for these jobs. Having got ourselves all spruced up, we lined up for the inspection in the workshop area. Then there was a short delay while those who did not pass muster put the complaint right. It was just starting to get hot when we marched off to the location about a mile away. From a distance we saw some of our comrades marching past the great man. It was quite impressive, and amongst ourselves we discussed how best we could present ourselves on a par with infantry regiments who were drill-minded. Each of us just vowed to do his best.

A field is hardly the best place for a parade ground, but this area was the best place available. There were no concrete places or indeed parade grounds of any description, so we had to make the best of whatever we had. The Royal Engineer had given this field quite a lot of attention with their bulldozers and equipment to flatten it out level, and harden the surface. Fortunately, there had been no rain; if there had been, the show (and a show it was) would have been a lot different.

We waited in the sidelines for an age, ultimately being called on at about three o'clock in the afternoon. Then, having got ourselves properly lined up, we were marched on and gave a smart 'eyes right' as we passed the great man. I felt that we did a fairly good job. Certainly Major Dickie was pleased at the conclusion, and that was the most important point of all. Back in camp, the Major declared the canteen open, and we celebrated in the only way a soldier really knows.

We also celebrated in the Sergeants' Mess. We had no sorrows as such to drown, so we just drank a lot. Finally, in an attempt to remain sober, one of those present, Staff Sergeant McGregor, decided that he knew the only way to remain in good order. He produced a bucket of water and an apple, then calmly announced that nobody could have another drink until he had lifted the apple out of the water without using his hands.

In turn we all attempted to get the apple out. Don Gisby, the oldest of our members, was the only one to succeed. I tried and tried again, but without good result. Finally, Staff Sergeant McGregor decided to show us how it was done. Sure enough, he put his head straight in and lifted out the apple. We all accused him of cheating, which he denied quite emphatically.

While this denial was going on some of us put a handful of sand into the bucket. Then we all demanded, 'Let's see you do it again', and put more sand in the bucket. No problem. He put his head into the bucket and immediately came up with the apple and a mouthful of sand. We all agreed thereafter that he would be known as Dredger McGregor, a nickname that stuck with him for the rest of 'our war'.

Following General Eisenhower's inspection of the Division, there was a general feeling of relaxation everywhere. I paid visits to past locations, Kelibia was the first. Batiste was still there, and very happy to see me again. There, we had an alfresco meal of octopus and fish outside his hut, and a bottle of wine that went down extremely well. The same day, 5th September, I also had an extended visit to Nabeul. There I watched some of the artisans working away at old brass shell cases, making ashtrays and other items that they engraved with all manner of messages, crests and badges. I bought a few gifts to send home to my parents and friends.

Limbo In Tunisia

That night the Sergeants' Mess cook decided in his wisdom, and to our complete surprise, to make some pastry, but did not have a pastry roller. I told him that was no excuse, and went out and cut off a piece of wood from an olive tree. I took this to the machinery lorry and turned him a pastry roller. He was both surprised and very happy, and immediately set about making up some pastry for us to eat that night, unusual pastry that was well received all round. Thereafter, our pastry roller did a great deal of work that we all appreciated.

There were no German troops in North Africa now. Thankfully, they had long since departed. However, walking round the workshop, taking in everything that was going on, one could be excused for thinking that they were still here. It seemed that all the regiments we serviced had been sending in any small job, just to have the slate clean. It did not worry us, but quite clearly something was going on and equally clearly, we were not going to be left at the nice and easy location of Hammamet forever.

On 19th October, I was pleased to receive an invitation from the 19th Field Regiment, Royal Artillery, to a boxing match and drinks at the Regimental Headquarters. I rarely turned down such invitations, not that they came in all that often, but it was a way the regiments had of thanking us for the work we had done on their equipment.

The boxing was good, and I was most impressed by the talent of my good friend, Battery Sergeant Major Badgie Johnson. I am alluding to his ability at boxing; he was truly a master of the art, and most interesting to watch. It was appreciated by all present. After this we all made our way to the Sergeants' Mess at Regimental Headquarters, where the drinks, chatter and camaraderie were wonderful.

Not only did I make many good friends at this get-together, but it was obvious that my work in the workshop had been appreciated by the Gunners as well as the Sergeants and Officers.

I was approached to give a lecture to the Limber Gunners, just to ensure that they kept their guns in tip-top condition and working order. Not a bad idea, I thought. What a pity they had not got someone who knew the business to give me a lecture in the London Welsh, when I was their very green Limber Gunner a few years back.

I accepted the invitation, but soon found that I was not an expert lecturer. It is, after all, something that has to be learned, and I satisfied myself with that thought. I decided to teach myself and perhaps learn by my own mistakes. I did at least have a captive audience who were all interested in the subject - probably because they had avoided a fatigue of some sort by being there! My lecture went down well with the officers, and I also learned a lot about myself. Yes, it went down so well that I soon found myself being called upon to lecture the Limber Gunners of most of the Divisional Artillery over the following days. So popular were these talks that I was then asked to give a talk on the seventeen-pounder anti-tank gun. This was a gun that was quite new to me, but I did at least have a handbook.

The workings of the seventeen-pounder were in many ways similar to our old friend the twenty-fiive-pounder, although its use was somewhat different. The talk went down well, and I made many new friends.

Having done a number of jobs outside normal armament section work for the Divisional Convalescent Depot, we were suddenly asked to produce a football team. We gladly accepted the invitation, and we played against them on their depot grounds on 30th October, 1943. I was a little worried about their team, as they had four professional footballers; even our top man, Stan Jones, an ex-pro footballer himself, was a little worried. Thankfully, Stan was a professional goalkeeper in peace time and we drew one- one with the Con Depot, so honours were even all round.

Nabeul always held a strange fascination for me. I was impressed by the way the various Arab artisans went about their work before the public, and my admiration for the way they worked never ceased. My last trip to Nabeul was on 17th November, 1943, and I walked there and back from Hammamet. I looked forward to watching these people work on my way there, and was full of admiration for them on my return journey. They worked with very basic, almost ancient tools, but their finished articles were admirable.

There was no doubt in anyone's mind at this time that we would be moving to somewhere distant very soon. We had done all of the normal clear-up work, then we started getting orders to waterproof vehicles again. The last time we had done this had been for a brief landing of certain units on Pantalaria. This time the options were similar. It had to be Italy or France. I still had the hammock that I had made back in Kilmarnock prior to our move to North Africa. I brought it out and checked it over. The old piece of canvas that I used was in good condition. I could sleep well on the move.

PART FOUR

The Move To Italy

On 20th November, 1943, we left Hammamet at 4pm and drove to Bizerta, where we remained overnight. I slept in my hammock in the machinery lorry, and was very comfortable. The following day we moved a few miles to another location and remained there until the morning of Sunday, 5th December, when we drove on to an L.S.T., a landing ship tank, a massive steel structure with the most comfortable bunk-beds I have ever seen.

Shortly after midday on 6th December, 1943, the ship left Bizerta. I went up on deck to marvel at the view, and at three o'clock saw Pantaleria in the distance. After a very fine meal, I retired to my bunk and read a book. The following morning, we passed Pantalaria and could see Malta in the distance. The sea was calm and the weather beautiful. In fact, everything was good, and all we had to do was enjoy the generally relaxed feeling and good food of the ship.

On 9th December, we were travelling up the side of Sicily and saw Mount Etna. The following morning we approached Taranto and docked there at five o'clock in the afternoon. From there we made our way to a staging post nearby. I was amazed to see a great many Italians, all attempting to sell various souvenirs of the country. I was beginning to like my hammock, and left once again hung up like a bat in the machinery lorry.

On 12th December, we moved to another staging camp a little further inland. We were told that this was only a short stop-over, and we would be on the move the following morning. Sure enough, we moved off early in the morning of 13th December, and this time it seemed that we were going to travel some distance. We even travelled through the night. I was certainly getting full value out of the old piece of canvas that I had picked up in Kilmarnock way back. I could not get over how useful and comfortable my hammock turned out to be.

Spinazola

On the morning of 15th December, we arrived at the station yard in the town of Spinazola. At least there we had hard standing, and the town looked as if it could be interesting. Apart from checking over our own equipment, there seemed to be little work to do here.

We spent some time making sure that all of our equipment and vehicles were in tip-top working order. My main task was to attempt to learn Italian. I found the language lent itself easily to my tongue, and the locals in this quaint little town were most friendly and anxious to speak to us. With my little pocket dictionary and a lot of patience, I managed to pick up quite a lot, and held short conversations that were actually understood.

I also found that these local people were most hospitable, more so than I had ever discovered before. They truly welcomed us into their homes. They enjoyed their food, and were honoured if you would come and share it with them.

Christmas day came, and to the very obvious pleasure of the troops, the Sergeants and some of the Officers turned out to serve up the Christmas dinner and clean up afterwards. A good time was had by all, and our efforts were appreciated. The trouble was that this was indeed too good to be true. I found myself again asking the burning question: 'Is this the lull before the storm?' It just had to be.

I was really beginning to like Italy and the people. I found the language easier than French, and the Italians we met clearly wanted to be friendly. Nevertheless, nice as they appeared to us, we were still very wary and on our guard with them. Two big things were foremost in our minds: the Germans were on the run, and we were now at least going in the right direction - towards home. Despite all this, my principal worry at the time was that I was now twenty-three years old. Would I still get into the police after the war, or would I be too old when it did actually end?

The town of Spinazola was quaint, and I was sorry to leave it. I had made a number of friends and learned a lot, but we were on the move again, and I had a job to do. At 9pm on New Year's day, 1944, we moved out of the railway yard and were off to our next location. There was no indication as to where it would be, but we knew that it was some distance.

The following morning, one of the vehicles broke down. It was petrol trouble, and many excuses were put forward. I did not get involved in this matter, and suffice to say that the petrol system of the vehicle had to be stripped down, and we were on the move again in about two hours. The culprit was thought to be the petrol that we had picked up in gerry cans. Furthermore, we reckoned that there had been water in the petrol. More vigilance would be needed when recharging petrol tanks in future. We'd already had orders to use funnels with a filter incorporated when recharging petrol tanks. Clearly, 'someone' had ignored this important instruction and poured petrol directly into the tank of the vehicle.

Fianno

At 6.20 in the evening of 2nd January, 1944, we arrived at the foot of a hill leading to a hilltop village called Fianno. We camped at the side of the road on hard standing, and put up tents in a field beside our vehicles. After work the following day, I went up the hill to the village of Fianno. There I found a barber's shop, which was full. A barber was busy cutting one man's hair, but everyone in the premises was gossiping. I felt I could do with a haircut, so went inside. I was welcomed profusely, but insisted upon waiting my turn. This rather surprised them. It was clear to me that they expected me to demand to be served immediately.

I was drawn into conversation, and found once again that I was able to communicate with Italians without too much difficulty. In due course my turn came for a haircut. It was quite an experience. Time seemed no object, and the barber just wanted to do a job that pleased me and the audience of villagers present. He gave me a haircut and attention that would have cost me a small fortune in the West End of London.

There were no embarrassing questions about what we were doing in their village, or where we were going. I was impressed. The barber, who would not take any money, later brought out a bottle of wine and some glasses. Needless to say, the wine was soon gone.

Before leaving, Simon (an unusual name for an Italian), one of the villagers, asked me to come back to his house with him, and to meet his wife and have a meal. It was a very nice invitation, but I told him I was on duty in the camp that evening. I mentioned, however, that I could call on him the next day, if that was suitable. He agreed to my suggestion, and we parted company.

The next morning we were very busy in the workshop. There were a number of vehicles waiting to be waterproofed, and we set about that task once again. The rumour-mongers were having a field day. We were going to France. Why else would they give us such an easy pitch as this little village, which many of them had already sampled.

They had worked it all out. The next move would be to another L.S.T. that would drop us ashore in France. It all sounded just too logical to me, but the army does not always do logical things. It could be a possibility, but no more.

I paid a further visit to the barber's shop the next evening. Simon was delighted to see me. Did I like spaghetti? he asked. Frankly, I was not keen on spaghetti, because the only spaghetti I had ever tasted had been out of a tin in England, but I lied and said that I did. Together we moved off to his house at the edge of the village, looking over the valley where the workshop was parked.

Simon's wife was a charming woman. She produced a bottle of wine and three glasses then, after making sure that Simon and I were both comfortable, she got on with the cooking. Shortly after drinking the first glass of wine we were called to the table where I saw the biggest mountain of spaghetti I had ever seen, piled high on a huge plate. This was only for the three of us!

I was handed a plate heaped with spaghetti, on top of which the good lady poured a very healthy portion of meat sauce. This was spaghetti Bolognese, I was told. I had some difficulty getting the spaghetti on to the fork, but Simon showed me how to get over this problem with the aid of a spoon. I soon began to enjoy to the full my first true Italian meal of spaghetti.

The evening passed all too quickly for me. The food and company were most enjoyable. Then to cap it all, Simon insisted that I came again the following day. I assured him that this was not all that easy for me because I had a lot of work that I had to get on with in the workshop. I parted company with my friends with the promise to return at the first possible opportunity.

Back in the camp, more work was coming in, more vehicles to be waterproofed. This was big. If we were on to just a beach landing it had to be big, very big indeed.

We worked until the early hours of the morning, and as vehicles left us others came in. I think that we were by now quite convinced that it had to be France for our next stop. We remained in Fianno for nearly three weeks. It was hard work, but we had plenty of relaxation in between. We were also pleased to be doing work that was obviously useful to the war effort. Almost every day, I paid a visit to the village, or to Simon and his wife. It was even difficult at times to believe that there was a war on.

I was working with a team of lads when the order came through to move from Fianno. We stopped everything, packed our vehicles and moved out. It seemed to be a matter of urgency, for we did not stop until we arrived close to the docks at Castelamare in the Bay of Naples. It was 24th January, 1944, and as soon as we stopped we were directed to a particular L.S.T. and boarded. The following morning, we left Castelamare. The sea was very rough, and the noise that reverberated through the ship was as if the ship had been hit by shells.

Anzio

Once again our bunks were most comfortable. What worried most of us was the condition of the electric welding of the metal panels on the sides of the ship. The welds were so rough that they looked as if they had been made by trainees. Certainly my two welders, Croft and Westall, would never have produced welds like these. Had they done so, their work would have been rejected.

The noise in the ship had to be heard to be appreciated. The ship's bow would rise high in the air as it went over a wave, then crash down on the next wave with a shudder that would pass right through the vessel. How the ship remained in one piece was a marvel to us all. We were in a small convoy of ships including two other L.S.T.s.

Suddenly I noticed that we had veered off from the convoy. I asked one of the seamen, 'What's going on? We've left the convoy.'

His reply said many things. 'Don't worry, soldier, this tub steers by twin screws at the after end; one has got blocked or something. When the engineers put it right we'll join the convoy again.' He then turned and left to go below.

There was nothing I could do in any event. I remained on deck and could see flashes of gunfire in the distance. I was pleased to see that the ship had turned towards the convoy after about an hour. It did not look as if it was going to catch up with the other ships, and my thoughts went back to the tales we had heard of stragglers in convoys falling foul of the German U-Boats. I just hoped that there was none in our area.

While this was going through my mind, I suddenly found that we were being shelled from the shore. Guns were firing from some of the ships in the convoy near us. Some enemy shells roared over our heads, others thankfully fell short. We had now arrived at the port of Anzio, and Lady Luck had clearly been with us during our journey. We all prayed silently that she would remain with us for a while yet.

Then, while I was deep in thought, or perhaps prayer, there was a very loud bump and we were all thrown forward sharply. This was followed by a grinding sound. We had hit the beach.

It was late on 27th January, when we docked at the port of Anzio. The bow doors were opened, and we left the ship, driving up the beach into Anzio town. Here I saw a most surprising thing. Bill Bailey, a Sergeant in the Divisional Provost Company, was standing on a large box, directing traffic. He was certainly earning his pay! The whole area around us was one of devastation from bombs and shelling, and the distant and not so distant noise of gunfire added menace to the atmosphere.

We followed the directions of the Military Police through the town, which was being shelled at the time. The whole place was in such a mess. We then turned towards the sea, and continued along the coast road. We were glad to leave the town, or what was left of it, behind. Whole buildings were going up in smoke and shells were dropping far closer than was good for anyone's health. Once out of the town, we felt a little safer, but only a little. At least the shells were going past us. We could hear them whistling overhead and crashing into the town. Our main worry was that we were driving directly at the guns. We could actually see the flash as they fired. This was an extremely noisy welcome to Anzio.

After what seemed a very short distance, perhaps just over a mile, I found that we were getting nearer and nearer to the explosions of shells that were obviously coming our way.

We turned into a yard. We were indeed happy to pull our vehicles into the surrounds of what had once been very large brick kiln, where the walls at the base were at least ten feet thick. Major Dickie called us all together for a meeting. At the entrance of the kiln was what had once been an office. We parked the machinery lorries near the entrance, and put the electric welding equipment on the other side of the area that would comprise the main workshop area. The kiln proper was in the centre of the kiln surround. This was some fourteen feet thick at the base.

As for sleeping accommodation, there were a number of built-in rooms in the surrounding wall that had probably been offices or storerooms. These were allocated to various groups. Walking round the outside of the surround, I found a room that faced south towards the town. This I took for myself and the Instrument Mechanic Artificer, Staff Sergeant 'Shalom' Gaffin. This was very comfortable, but the noise and flashes of explosions during the night were quite shocking. Thus sleep did not come that easily, even tired as we were.

The following morning we were up at first light, and after a quick wash and shave, went in search of the cookhouse. Like ourselves, the cooks had not slept well, but were on the job early as usual. The food was good by army standards, and we were at least glad to be eating together. We had, over the past couple of years, been accustomed to powdered egg, powdered milk and bread with the inevitable weavil. Despite all this, most of us were quite fit and ate well.

After breakfast, several vehicles came in for repair. Some had been in accidents, others were badly shot up. We all turned out to get them back on the road very quickly. While this was going on, shells were exploding around us about a hundred yards away. That worried me a little. I say 'a little' ironically, because above the camp was an American ninety-millimetre gun site, and between our workshop and the gun site was a large ammunition dump. Our main worry was that if one of the attacking shells hit that dump, there would have been an extremely large explosion indeed, an explosion that would have utterly devastated our workshop.

We managed to turn the vehicles round as they came in for repair, and send them back to their regiments. When they had all gone off, Tiny Morris, the A.S.M., called all of the Senior N.C.O.s together and walked us out to a hut next to the ammunition dump. It had been a store hut for the kiln and was quite large. Tiny had taken possession of it as the Sergeants' Mess, and we set about collecting a few tables and chairs to make it more homely.

One wag amongst us pointed out to Tiny that there was a great pile of ammunition only about ten yards from the hut, and did he think it would be a good idea to have the Mess there? Our A.S.M. smiled and said, 'If a shell does hit it, we'll never hear it, so why worry?' We all laughed, perhaps hollowly, but it was agreed that this was now our Sergeants' Mess.

The bombing and shelling continued day and night, and work continued to come in. Clearly our twenty-five-pounders were doing a great job, for from the armament section angle they kept my lads very busy indeed. Then on 31st January, there was a lot of shelling and bombing in the area. Also at this time there were a strange series of explosions above us. These were not 'air bursts' but what we later nicknamed the efforts of 'Anzio Archie'. The Germans had a very large gun hidden away in the hills and when it fired it sounded more like a clang than a bang. Then shortly after the clang, there would be an explosion above us. The next thing we knew would be a really massive explosion in Anzio town, and a cloud of rubble and smoke would rise from where the shell had landed.

Strategic Background

By late October 1943 the Allied advance through Italy had ground to a halt a bare seventy miles north of Salerno, where they had landed in September. The geography of the country was well suited to defence, and the Germans had built a formidable defence right across the peninsular. The Gustav Line was a masterpiece of fortifications, bristling with traps, concrete gun-emplacements and barbed wire. Its pivot was the mountain mass of Casino, which completely dominated the lines towards Rome. This situation led to the decision to try and break the stalemate by mounting a flanking seaborne assault at Anzio on 22-23 January 1944.

Extract from 'The Reme Journal' ~ Spring 1999.

This was not a place for the faint-hearted. Many of the lads who had taken refuge at night in the small rooms around the kiln started digging themselves a dugout where they could perhaps sleep more easily. With our workshop in the kiln being such a large building, I was surprised that the Germans had not decided in their wisdom to flatten it. What would have made the workshop more visible to the Germans was the constant use of electric welding equipment; their watchers must have seen the frequent flashes made by the machinery.

During one of my inspections of the surrounds of the kiln area, I found an old quarry truck, one of those quaint carriers used in quarries that run on rails and can be tipped sideways by knocking off the retaining catches from their locked position. This was going to be the roof of my dugout. I showed it to my friend Shalom, and we started digging ourselves a decent-sized dugout. We went down six feet and shuttered up the sides with odd pieces of wood found in the area, making ourselves very comfortable. We had two bunks, and an area at one end where we could brew up. It was great.

The following morning, there was a great deal of air activity. Hundreds of American bombers flew over us and dropped their bombs about a mile from us. The ground shook, and the smoke rose high in the air. If it came from the German lines, they had little pity from me. At least I was glad we were not at the mercy of such raids by the Luftwaffe. Perhaps this would keep the harassing fire from the German guns quiet.

This was indeed a very noisy place, but in the comparative safety of our dugout, sleep came in time. Sometimes we slept soundly, sometimes not so soundly. I did not drink in those days, as I was still smarting from the lesson I had learned with the French Foreign Legion lads in Tunis. The trouble was that at this particular time, we even had a rum issue, which I kept for a weak moment. When the time came, I found that swigging a tot of rum in my sleeping bag really helped me to fall into a nice sound sleep.

The trouble with drink, though, is that you get used to it. At first, one shot of rum gave me a wonderful night's sleep. I heard nothing, and believe me, that was some feat in such a noisy place. But after a while one shot did very little for me, so I took another, and soon it was three before I sank into the arms of Morpheus. I soon realised that the false confidence given by 'Nelson's blood', as we used to call rum, was likely to do me more harm than good. I had given up *zibbib* in North Africa, now I gave up rum.

Work continued to come in as fast as we managed to get it out, and we did not stop at all: twenty-five-pounders, six-pounder anti-tank guns, and seventeen-pounders, we never seemed to be without them. The seventeen-pounders had a problem. We had to modify and fix muzzle brakes to them and my turner, Jim Wilkinson on the big lathe, was kept very busy indeed.

To those of us experienced in field artillery guns, all these modifications of muzzle brakes prompted the big question: why? This was a tried and tested gun that had apparently proved itself most satisfactory under normal circumstances.

The answer came from a number of angles. One of the most impressive came from one of the Gunners who had brought in the first seventeen-pounder for the modification. He had fired the gun at a German Tiger tank. The shell had hit the tank, made a loud clang and bounced off! The tank turned and the second shot destroyed the tank. This tank had heavier armour plate fitted than had previously been seen by this regiment, and so they had asked for a heavier charge to be used. The muzzle brakes had to be modified in order to restrict the gun's recoil after firing the increased charge. This sounded all very logical, but I never did hear the true reason for the sudden change of muzzle brakes.

It was with one of these modifications that I had my first spot of Union trouble. I had been asked how long it would take to carry out each modification and, since I did not want to guess, I started timing Jim Wilkinson with his muzzle brake. He switched off his lathe and said, 'Don't do that to me, Mr Swain.' Then he explained, 'I'm sorry, but please listen to me. When I see any time study work being carried out, I find myself thinking back to when I was a lad, and the owner would grind us into the ground with the times given by the time study engineer. Just leave me alone, and I'll tell you how long it takes; nobody will do the job quicker.'

He had a point that was not quite in line with military discipline, but he did a wonderful job on those brakes, and his work was greatly appreciated all round. They were all fitted on time, and I later heard that our seventeen-pounders accounted for a great number of German armoured vehicles in our push to Rome.

During the night of 17th February, there was a continuous period of enemy shelling, with shells getting so close that I sincerely hoped our hole in the ground was the best place to be. When I went to get water to wash the following morning, I was told that a shell had hit one of the rooms on the edge of the kiln, killing two of the lads. It was a very sad day indeed, and when we looked at the shell and bomb holes around our camp, we realised that we were extremely lucky not to have had more casualties.

My Near Demise

By the time I had washed and shaved, the workshop was full of guns and vehicles that had arrived for repair, and we set to work once again to get them back in action.

The night of 24th February, 1944 is one that I will never forget. It had been an exceptionally noisy day. There had been huge waves of American bombers again, and sporadic shelling of our area. I finally climbed into our dugout and got into bed after a good drink in the Sergeants' Mess. I was happy in the knowledge that I had the old quarry truck above me, although a direct hit would have ended that happiness.

The night was noisy, but with the aid of what I had drunk in the Mess, I was soon asleep. I was suddenly awoken by what I thought was a large explosion that had shaken the dugout. Shalom was also awake. He called out to me, 'Did you hear that, John?' I said I had not heard anything, but thought I had been shaken. We soon stopped talking, and were off to sleep again.

I got up at first light as usual, and climbed out of the dugout to get some water to wash and shave. On the Anzio town side of the dugout lay a German 88mm shell. I looked on the other side of the dugout and saw a hole or indentation in the ground. It looked as if the shell had gone into the ground on the north side, come up on the town side of the dugout, then come to rest about twenty feet from the dugout entrance.

I called Shalom to come out and have a look at what I had found. He came out and I showed him what looked like the entry point of the shell on one side of the dugout, and a disturbed depression in the ground on the other side which looked like an exit point. He put his hands together and muttered some words in Hebrew that I could not understand. I watched in interest. When he had finished, he turned to me and said, 'Well, John, don't you think you should say a few words to your bloke as well?' I told him that I believed our shell had landed on one side of the dugout and bounced over it without exploding, and I should indeed thank the Lord.

The more I thought about the closeness of our demise, the more I found myself looking at the dugout and imagining what the scene would have looked like had that shell exploded. I would now have been gazing into a huge crater - if I had been around to gaze at all. It was a not a nice feeling.

I had to shake it off. Somehow it did not seem right that the shell could have entered the sandy ground and come up so quickly in so short a space, about thirty feet, after going down some eight feet and clearing the bottom of the dugout. I came up with the only conclusion that seemed logical: the shell had hit the ground on one side of the dugout, bounced over the quarry truck roof of the dugout, and come to rest where I found it. The real miracle, of course, was that the thing had not exploded when it hit the ground in the first place. Silent prayers of thanks seemed in order. We had been lucky, damned lucky, and we expressed our thanks in the only way open to us.

There was sadness in the workshop at the loss of our two comrades a few nights earlier. As for our escape, as far as the Mess was concerned, having suffered a near-direct hit once, our dugout had to be the safest place in the camp area. Lt Geoff Dowler RN, a regular visitor, hastened to assure all present that, according to Dowler's Law of Probability, it was most unlikely that there would be a second direct hit. That was his line of logic, and the odds were in favour of it.

It was at about this time that a hut, familiar in design, was suddenly erected outside our camp on the top of the cliff by some naval personnel. Then a peculiar antenna was erected. I thought this new arrival looked similar to one which had appeared at the Westminster Bank Sports Ground when I had first joined up in 1939. I was right: it turned out to be a radar or radio location monitoring station.

This operation was under the direction of Lt. Geoff Dowler RN.

Anzio

This small naval outpost had been placed in this selected position to watch over the movements of ships, particularly German E-Boats, around the mouth of the River Tiber to the north of our position. Lt. Geoff Dowler RN was in charge of this outpost, and he proved to be quite a lad. After propounding his Laws of Probability and announcing his ruling on our dugout, he rested his case and suggested that it was time we all had a game of cards, just to cheer the place up.

I was all for this, as were most of the others. We all had money because we had nowhere to spend it. 'What shall we play?' was the next cry. Someone suggested 'Shoot', otherwise known as 'Slippery Sam', and there were other suggestions. There followed a discussion as to which game was the best, and I attempted to break up this chatter up by expressing my interest in the radar shack, explaining to Geoff Dowler that I had been interested in this since seeing my first one in England, when it was referred to as G.L.

I was actually privileged to watch Geoff's men plotting the movement of these E-Boats, and seeing attacks on them launched by our Navy. Radio location, G.L. or radar had come a long way since I had last inspected such a piece of equipment back in 1939.

But back to the card game. I had never heard of 'Shoot' before, but went along with the quorum, and 'Shoot' it was. We played this stupid game until the early hours of the morning, and when I had lost more money than I had ever done before, I retired with Shalom to our now 'safe' dugout.

On 9th March, Lt. Scofield, decided that he would have to break up the armament and vehicle sections into squads. I had no idea what had prompted this move, and could not see any point to it. It was then that I learned that our lines of communication had been badly stretched by the German activity. Therefore, in order to prevent German breakthrough into our sector, we were going to put men in the line to help block off any attempted breakthrough. After that, a squad of eight men would periodically leave the camp to take up a set defensive position.

In early March my friend, Sergeant Bob Phillips of the Field Security Section, had trouble with his motorcycle. I had it taken into the workshop, where we did the necessary repairs. He was delighted, and invited me to their headquarters, which were close to our workshop, for a very convivial evening. One interesting point was made during that evening: how much our eight men in the line had pleased the already heavily taxed infantrymen of 2nd Brigade.

It was about this time that an unusually high number of men went sick with some ailment or other. Every morning, we had to queue up for Mepacrin tablets, which were supposed to prevent bouts of malaria and sand-fly fever. Many of the lads went a little yellow as a result of taking these tablets. Despite such measures, we still had too many going off sick. Furthermore, the incidence of these complaints affected the whole of the forces on the Anzio Beachead.

The seriousness of so many soldiers reporting sick demanded action from the top. As far as the workshop was concerned, it was Lt. Scofield who again came up with a plan of action. The whole of our camp area had to be sprayed with anti-malaria spray, and certain areas were allocated for the men to spray thoroughly.

In a field beside the Field Security building, I saw Bob Phillips with one of these sprays and went over to talk with him. South of Anzio were the Pontine Marshes, and apparently they were suspected of being a breeding ground for all manner of bugs. They were also considered a serious hazard because of the high incidence of malaria there in peacetime. Therefore, all areas adjoining the marshes were to be sprayed, each regiment being responsible for the area that they occupied. Bob Phillips was thus responsible for an area of some ten acres, which he had to spray regularly.

He told me that he would soon be finished and, indicating a small tree, said, 'When I've finished, come over to that tree and see me.' I returned to the workshop. About half an hour afterwards, I could not see Bob Phillips in the field, so I went to the place he had indicated. By this tree he had bent a branch to make a seat, and was sitting there reading a book.

We chatted away about the war, and things in general. Suddenly I saw a large snake about six feet long slithering past us with its head in the air. 'Leave it alone, it won't hurt you,' said Bob. 'It's poisonous for sure, but won't harm you unless you interfere with it.' It was sound logic, and I was not likely to interfere with such a reptile. I happily watched it depart.

We met at Bob's arbour on many occasions, and used to look out to sea to see the ships arriving and leaving Anzio. I was with him there on one occasion when a large American battleship was shelling the German lines. The shells were going over our heads, making a noise like an express train. This was followed by a very loud explosion behind us in the not-so-distant German lines.

Work was still coming in in large doses. The guns were firing very regularly, and needed to be repacked and have many different repairs done to them. I even had a 5.5-inch Gun Howitzer in for a barrel change. That really did cause a stir. I was one of the few people who had ever seen the guts of this monster, and then only at the Military

College of Science. Despite my minor worries, we got the job done and sent it on its way to cause more trouble to the German Army, now hopefully on its way home and to the north of us.

Late in May, 1944, my friend Jock Bennett, the Artificer Sergeant Major in charge of the R.E.M.E. L.A.D. (Light Aid Detachment) attached to the 67th Field Regiment, Royal Artillery came into the workshop to get some electric welding done on one of his guns.

I examined the gun and found a number of rivets which had worked loose, and the gun limber needed patching up as well. While I was arranging for the work to be done, Jock asked me if I would like to visit one of his gun emplacements. This was an opportunity I could not turn down, particularly as I was well aware that the guns were now very busy on what was hoped would be the last barrage before Rome.

This was something I had wanted to do before. I had been asked on many occasions, but had always been far too busy with work in hand. This, however, was a heaven-sent opportunity at just the right time. My friend had a Jeep and promised to take me to the gun position by way of Carroceto, bringing me back to my workshop, later. I could not refuse this offer.

We drove through what was left of Carroceto and the ruins of Aprilia. There was so little left of these two very small towns. We drove past the famous tobacco factory, the flyover and the railway embankment, all notorious battlegrounds during the recent months. The strange smell of death was with us throughout this journey, a haunting smell that I had not experienced since passing through Medjez el Bab back in North Africa. It is an odour you never forget.

We finally stopped close to a Battery of 67th Field Regiment twenty-five-pounder guns that were engaged in a harassing fire barrage. We visited each gun pit and the command post, and met some of the characters I had drunk with back in Kilmarnock, before we left England back in 1943.

The guns were firing regularly, typical harassing fire, and we bid our friends goodbye and drove off. As we drew near to the workshop, we could hear the regular firing of the twenty-five-pounders. Then one explosion sounded a lot louder than the rest. 'That sounds as if Gerry has hit our ammunition dump,' said Jock. And we continued on our way.

The following day, Jock Bennett called again at the workshop. He told me that the German artillery had made a direct hit on one of the gun emplacements we had visited, killing some of the crew. I said a silent prayer for our departed comrades and offered thanks to Lady Luck, who had once again protected us. We had been in the actual gun pit that had been hit, and could well have been there when the terrible thing happened. Back at camp all the talk was about the battle for Casino being over. General Mark Clarke and his men had moved on. We had heard so much about the battle for Casino, the monastery, Mount Casino, and the difficulties encountered there.

Permission was given for four of us to take a fifteen hundredweight truck and visit the area. In this battle, despite the combined efforts of the Allied Forces, the Germans had retained hold of Monte Casino and the monastery until the last moment. Here the vast expanse of destroyed dwellings told the whole story. To cap it all, on top of Monte Casino was a massive heap of rubble that had once been the famous Casino Monastery.

In early June 1944, Rome had been taken, and there was a march past in front of General Mark Clarke of the American Fifth Army. Mark Clarke had been stuck at Casino south of Anzio for months. At Anzio, we kept receiving radio messages such as 'Mark Clarke will be with you in eight hours', 'Mark Clarke will be with you tomorrow'. It got to the stage when we all wondered whether Mark Clarke knew exactly what was going on. Whoever had sent them must have been known to the General. To us it was very unreal.

Our workload was getting smaller, and we therefore set about getting our house, or rather our workshop, in order. We were told to get ready to move out and waited patiently for the word. It seemed a long time coming. Shalom and I were still very comfortable in our dugout, but that had to come to an end soon. Thankfully, I still had my hammock in the machinery lorry for when we started off on the move again.

I think it was late in June when we finally received the order to move out. We were all very happy at the thought of getting to Rome. The roads on the way were in a terrible state, however. With the heavy vehicles that we had, the journey was fraught with difficulties. Bomb and shell holes were numerous. The sides of the roads were for the most part unsafe, and there was the ever present stench of death. Notwithstanding this, we were useful in our way. We found a number of vehicles from other units that had fallen foul of these bad roads and rescued them, repairing some on the spot and putting others on tow immediately to take along with us.

Rome

We ended up at what was to be known to us all as the Exhibition Buildings on the Ostia Lido Road, west of Rome These buildings had been erected before the war for an exhibition that never took place. Here we were billeted in proper buildings with an area reserved for workshop use. We were very happy here. Yes, there was plenty of work to be done, but we knew that Rome was an open city, and as such would not be subjected to air bombardment. There was no bombing or shellfire here, and there was the promise of plenty of leave to add to the overall feeling of wellbeing.

Here we experienced the not-so-nice side of the Italian people. On our second evening, there was an outcry. All nations have their thieves, but this was the first and only experience we had of them in Italy. Three men had walked into the workshop area on the blind side of a Jeep that was in for repair. They had lifted the Jeep up and stolen two of the wheels. Fortunately they were caught as they walked off with the wheels, rolling them along like children's hoops. They were handed over to the Military Police, who passed them on to the civilian authorities to deal with.

We in the workshop, however, were given quite a talking to by the Military Police for allowing this to happen. Furthermore, Major

Dickie was not pleased, and a proper picket was put in place after that.

The Exhibition Buildings were in a wonderful location, close to Rome, with comfortable sleeping accommodation and adequate workshop facilities. We were going to take advantage of this situation and enjoy our stay, even though work continued to pour in. That was something that really surprised us. The regiments of the Division had advanced north of Rome, but they had been obliged to leave a lot of equipment for us to repair: evidence, clearly, that the Division had taken a hammering during the campaign of the Anzio Beachhead.

I was soon taking advantage of our close proximity to Rome. I had a liking for the Cafe Pagani in the Via Nationale. Here chairs and tables were set out on the pavement and in the peaceful warmth of the approaching summer, it was great to sit there and sup a nice drink of whatever took your fancy. It also gave me the opportunity to try out my scant knowledge of Italian, which needed a lot of brushing up. The Cafe Pagani was within very comfortable walking distance from the Victor Emmanuel Monument, the Colosseum and the Ancient Fuoro d'Italia. I found the historical buildings of Italy fascinating. I also found the Italians themselves to be most helpful and sociable, very much reminiscent of Simon and his wife back at Fianno.

Life here was one long round of work and pleasure. I often wondered whether it was supposed to be. Still, we worked hard, damned hard. The hours of the day made little difference to us, for we knew that if we cleared the work in hand to the satisfaction of all concerned, a period of rest or leave would follow. The Ostia Lido beach was only a few miles away, west of our location, and a vehicle was regularly available to take us there for a swim.

Caldini

Swimming at Ostia Lido was a little messy. The sand was black, and with it sticking to your feet as you came out of the water, they really looked dirty. Happily, however, by the time we'd washed them and got back to camp, we did feel really clean, which was the primary object of the exercise.

We were kept so busy with our work and visits to Rome that it only seemed a few days before we were packing up to move again. On 5th August, 1944, we moved away from the Exhibition Buildings and Rome. We passed through Perugia and stopped at Arezzo, a very striking location on the side of a hill.

On 7th August, we moved on to San Giovanni for an overnight stop. Here we made new Italian friends, but were soon on the move again at 2am. This time we ended up at an Italian village called Caldini, north of Florence, in the early hours of 9th August.

Here we parked our vehicles in the railway station approach, and to my complete surprise we were allocated 'civvy billets' later that day. I had a room in a house, complete with a bed and mattress: I was going to enjoy this location and the sleeping facilities that went with it! It was all too good to be true. The Sergeants' Mess was set up in another house that was vacant, but that is another story.

Our guide to most of these empty houses was what we would call the village constable, an Italian police officer named Giorgio. He could not speak a word of English, but by this time my knowledge of Italian had expanded considerably, and we got on extremely well. On one occasion, during a chat, Giorgio indicated a large house at the end of the village. 'This would be a better place to set up your Sergeants' Mess,' he said. It certainly was larger than the one we were then using and it seemed a good idea.

The house, we found, was securely locked, and that surprised us. Something was not right. The owner, we were told, was not liked in the village, and had gone north with the Germans; he would not be welcomed back, should he ever decide to return. Clearly, the former occupier, whoever he was, had been sympathetic to the German cause, so we would probably be excused or even justified in seizing his house and using it as we wished. I thanked Giorgio for this information, but told him that I would have to discuss it with Major Dickie, who was in charge, before we took any action.

That afternoon, we had a visit from a Major in AMGOT - Allied Military Government. While he was talking to Major Dickie, A.S.M., Morris and me, I put the suggestion to the floor. The AMGOT Officer took up the matter immediately. 'Whatever you do, do not touch that house or anything in it,' he warned. 'You have been allocated accommodation. Other dwellings will be left strictly alone, and that, take it from me, is an order from the highest authority.'

There was, quite obviously more to this than we could ever have guessed, and we had no intention of disobeying orders. Major Dickie nodded in agreement, and the matter was forgotten. As it was, we were to a man quietly grateful for the unusual comfort that we were now beginning to enjoy in our new accommodation.

Shortly after the visit from the AMGOT Major, I was offered a week's leave in Rome to stay at the Rome Leave Camp. This was set up in buildings that had been prepared for the Olympic Games that never took place due to the war.

The Victor Emmanuel Moument, Rome ~ 1944.

It so happened that I'd received a letter from my father just before this period of leave. He had written to introduce me to a Captain Pollock, who had been a Police Officer in London, and had joined AMGOT. This sounded good.

Before leaving camp, I telephoned Captain Pollock. He was delighted to hear from me and, to my surprise and that of my colleagues, he sent a *carabiniere* officer to pick me up. The officer arrived in all his finery, driving a beautiful captured B.M.W. motorcycle and sidecar which had once been one of the German machine gun outfits. I don't know whether Captain Pollock had told the driver to get me to him fast, or whether the driver was trying to impress me, but I can assure you of one thing: he scared me stiff! We raced round Rome, cutting through side streets that he knew at a speed that would have had every policeman in London chasing him. Finally, and much to my relief, he stopped outside the Captain's office, and escorted me to his quarters.

Captain Pollock made me most welcome. I told him that I had a week's leave due to me in the near future and he promised me a visit to Rome that I would never forget. Shortly after this meeting, I was able to take up his offer.

Promises in wartime tend to be made in haste, and in the heat of the moment. They often cannot be kept because the service has other ideas, and you get posted far afield. But to my surprise, when my leave did come through, Captain Pollock was as good as his word.

The Massacre In Rome

As opposed to spending my time in a crowded military leave camp, I found myself set up in an apartment in the centre of Rome, which had probably been a high class boarding house before the war. Here I was really looked after. I slept between sheets, had my bed made up for me, and ate home-cooked Italian food. It was lovely, but very hard to get used to.

I had hardly settled in to this spacious abode when Captain Pollock decided to take me on a sightseeing tour of the city. He pointed out places of interest and other things that made me truly wonder where and how he had accumulated so much knowledge of this foreign city, especially as he hardly spoke a word of Italian.

One evening, he called to take me to a film show. I was not all that keen to sit in a cinema in the heat of Rome, and felt that there were better things to do in that city. I did attempt to find out what film he intended taking me to, but he would not give me a direct answer, other than to say that he thought I would enjoy it. Also, he felt that I could try out my knowledge of Italian on some of the things I saw.

I soon found out why he had been so vague. The film was for a large number of the top brass in the British, American, French

A.Q.M.S. Swain and A.S.M. Bennet in Rome, June 1944.

and even Polish armies, and it truly brought home to me the horrors of war.

Just outside the military barracks in Via Rasella in Rome, there had been an explosion. The area had been heavily patrolled by Germans after the Italian surrender and every day, thirty-two German soldiers assembled there at an exact time to begin their patrol. Italian partisans, no doubt local people, spotted the regularity of these patrols, and decided to take their own course of action. They planted a bomb timed to go off at the exact time when the patrol assembled. The bomb exploded on cue and wiped out the patrol. All thirty-two German soldiers were killed.

The German authorities were furious and decided to take action. They carried out an investigation, but got nowhere. Enquiries into this 'outrage', as the Germans called it, were led by the local Gestapo Chief, Herbert Kappler. He demanded that ten members of the local population should be executed for every German soldier killed. He sent for the local mayor, a man called Caruso, or something like that, who insisted that he knew nothing about the affair. Faced with their own failure to trace the culprits, the Germans told the mayor to produce a list of ten local inhabitants for every soldier killed. Caruso made out a list of three hundred and twenty people, which he passed on to Herbert Kappler.

Thereafter, the matter was dealt with by Kappler and S.S. Captain Erich Priebke. Those named were all arrested and taken to the Ardeatine Caves in groups. There, they were stripped of their valuables, marched further into the caves and shot; the caves were then blown in on top of these unfortunate people.

Captain Pollock had the job of investigating this terrible affair. In peacetime he was a London detective of some repute, and went about his task in a manner that truly proved his efficiency and ability. He filmed everything: interviews with people who could assist; the excavation of the caves and recovery of the bodies; the identification of the victims; the arrest of the one-time mayor, and the actual trial that followed.

It was known that Caruso was a much hated figure as a result of this atrocity, but the extent of that hatred had been underestimated by the authorities. At his trial, a large mob, similar to an American-style lynch mob, assembled outside the court. The authorities were unable to contain the crowd and, quite unexpectedly, they broke into the courtroom. The shock of this intrusion drew the attention of those in charge away from the prisoner, who immediately headed for a nearby window and leapt from it into the River Tiber that flowed past the building. Perhaps he believed that those in the mob were his friends. The mob, however, took to boats and went out after Caruso. When they caught up with him, they started beating him about the head with oars.

Fortunately, the authorities managed to step in and rescue the unfortunate man, and took him back to the courtroom. Thereafter, the trial took its normal course. Caruso was found guilty and sentenced to death by firing squad.

This was a film that I will never forget. The exact detail portrayed was vivid and true, without embellishments. I learned that there had been a considerable amount of bad feeling about which of the Allied soldiers would carry out the execution. The confusion was soon ironed out and Caruso was executed by a firing squad consisting of Italian Army personnel. The execution and *coup de grâce* were depicted in the film I refer to.

This whole matter proved to me that without doubt police experience could be channelled into some exceedingly interesting cases, whether in the army or civilian life. My avowed intention to join the Police when the war was over became even stronger.

I returned to my unit a wiser man, and very proud of the efforts of my father's friend, Captain Pollock. The extent of that investigation was difficult to put into words. It was vast and complex in the extreme, but he had done the right thing throughout. The filming of the investigation spoke volumes that would be difficult to put on paper. For me, an outsider looking in, the film explained everything. I remember all the Generals and senior military men who had been present at the screening. None of them had spoken, and as I watched them, it was obvious that they were seriously engaged in absorbing every aspect.

On 2nd September, 1944, I went with the leave truck to Florence. What a beautiful city it was, and how glad I was to see that it had not been subjected to the bombing that some other towns and cities had suffered. There was also a very nice Warrant Officers and Sergeants' Club in a building on the banks of the River Arno. Here drinks were very cheap, and the company of our comrades in arms wonderful.

Borgo San Lorenzo

Returning to Caldini, the routine of work and relaxation went on as before: plenty of work, but also plenty of time to ourselves. It had to come to an end, however. The end came on 26th September, 1944, quite out of the blue. I found myself posted to the 2nd Field Regiment, Royal Artillery, as the Acting Artificer Sergeant Major R.E.M.E., and given command of their Light Aid Detachment. This turned out to be only a temporary move. Even at the time, it seemed just too good to be true.

I was given a Jeep to get me to the Regimental Headquarters of the 2nd Field Regiment, and made my way to Maradi, where the R.H.Q. was situated. The R.H.Q. was in a large country house in an area that had to be fairly near to the German lines. Inside, however, it had been set up with offices and equipment that I did not expect to see so near the front. Here I met the Commanding Officer, Colonel Browne, and we had quite a long chat. The A.S.M. of the L.A.D. had gone off to an interview for a Commission. If he got through, my appointment would be confirmed. If not, I would be returned to my unit.

He gave me the exact location of the L.A.D. just outside Borgo San Lorenzo, and suggested that I might like to check it over and settle in. While we were talking, there were some of the loudest bangs I had heard since Anzio, explosions that were a lot closer than most of those I had previously heard in this area. The explosions were more of a loud crack than the resonant bang or boom of a shell exploding or firing. I looked at Colonel Browne and said, 'Somebody doesn't like us!'

He laughed and replied, 'That's a German mortar battalion. I think we'll know were they are now, and I'll be surprised if they remain in one piece in their present position for long.'

At that moment, I heard some artillery fire that I felt sure was from twenty-five-pounders. 'That sounds like your lads, Sir,' I said.

'Yes, that's them,' he replied. 'I think we can forget those damned mortars now.' I was introduced to the R.S.M. and two officers, then shortly afterwards made my way to Borgo San Lorenzo to examine just what I had taken over, and meet the men under my command. What an interesting location and job. There was plenty of work being done, mostly on vehicles, and the team of lads I would have working for me seemed good at their work. I spent a lot of time getting to know them, and the men of the regiment who were there with their equipment. I was enjoying the change and my new, exalted rank.

In the middle of October I was summoned to a meeting at the R.E.M.E. Headquarters to see Colonel Gorman (C.R.E.M.E.), the Commanding Officer of the Divisional R.E.M.E. I had no idea what he would want to see me for, and put it down to perhaps a regular meeting of those in charge of his Light Aid Detachments.

But this was not so. The Colonel greeted me in a warm, friendly manner. The A.S.M. in charge of 2nd Field Regiment, L.A.D. would be returning to his post. However, I was told not to worry, because there was going to be a vacancy for a new Commander of the 19th. Field L.A.D. and he wanted me for that job.

Colonel Gorman told me to report back to the 2nd Infantry Brigade Workshops, and assured me that I would be hearing from him in a few days. He also told me to retain my acting rank. This was all something of a come-down, but the fact that he had told me to retain my acting rank was very satisfying indeed. I returned to Caldini a little heavy-hearted, but with high hopes for the future.

Two days later, I was given a Movement Order to report to the Headquarters of the 19th Field Regiment, Royal Artillery. The regiment was located in support of the Monte Grande sector of the front line, south of Bologna. I made my way to the map reference given, some twenty miles north of Borgo San Lorenzo. Getting there, however, was not exactly an easy task. I had to travel over mountains, through narrow passes and across ravines where the retreating German army had blown up many roads and all of the bridges. Some journey! On this point, the Royal Engineers had come into their own. They built Bailey Bridges, most of which were under fire while being constructed.

These pieces of mechanical genius were named, in alphabetical order, Able, Baker, Charley, Dog Bridge etc. One, the largest of them all, always amazed me. I forget the actual name it had been given, but it was fondly referred to as the Assam Fu Bridge. I travelled over it on a number of occasions, and it was the longest of its type I had ever seen. It was heavily guarded, and the movement over it strictly controlled by our old friends the Military Police.

I recall that over a drink, on another occasion, I had asked one of the Royal Engineers the origin of this strange name. He told me that it was the name of the largest bridge ever built by the Royal Engineers at a place in Burma called Assam. This sounded like a fair explanation, and I accepted it probably in the same way as others before me had done.

On another occasion, however, I spoke to one of the engineers who had been involved in the whole project, and quite a different story came to light. Yes, Assam Fu was indeed the largest bridge this unit had ever built. It was built under almost constant shell fire from the enemy during its construction. Furthermore, due to the enemy attention and activity at the time, it had collapsed in part on a number of occasions. Hence the constant presence of the Military

Police to regulate the flow of traffic. And the name?

'No, my friend,' said the engineer, 'nothing to do with Burma. It stands for "A Self Adjusting Mechanical Foul Up", but we beat the bugger in the end.' This sounded more like it, though I never did bother to find out which explanation was true.

The Regimental Headquarters of 19th Field Regiment were only a few miles north of Assam Fu Bridge. The whole journey was treacherous to say the least. It was also very time-consuming. Many of the roads had been so damaged by earlier shellfire that normal two-wheel drive vehicles got stuck in the mud more often than not.

I did at least have a Jeep, but I had found yet another obstruction that involved travel time and had to be considered. Many of the supplies needed by the forward area troops were transported by mule train to the mountain areas. The Fourth and Eighth Indian Army Divisions were with us in this sector, and their ability to deal with the terrain was a lesson to us all. In addition we also had the Italian Mountain Troops, the Bersellieri, with their mules moving supplies for us.

All were dangers that had to be considered in travel. I assure you that driving an open Jeep past a mule train during shellfire and air activity is no fun at all. You cannot just drive past; you must learn to drive a little faster than the mule. Give it every consideration, then pass each one carefully, but very quickly, always remembering that they are all tied together.

I finally made 19th Field Regiment, Regimental Headquarters, and there I met Regimental Sergeant Major Hill, and Colonel Greig, the C.O. It was a very friendly meeting, and I was welcomed with open arms. They had received their report on me from Colonel Gorman, and were glad to have me in charge of their Light Aid Detachment.

The L.A.D. was set up in Borgo San Lorenzo, and I made my way there. I took over a disused garage, and began repairing the equipment of my new-found charge, the 19th Field Regiment, Royal

A.S.M. Swain.
Borgo San Lorenzo ~ September 1944.

Artillery. Work came in fast and furious, and thankfully the lads I had taken over in my new command worked well. At the same time, however, I felt that there was considerable loss of time in the operation. Before getting to the workshop, the equipment for repair had to travel over the extremely arduous terrain I have described. Then, on completion, it had to repeat that journey to get back to its place in the Regiment.

I made suggestions that the L.A.D. should move forward with the regiment, but this was refused point blank, despite my protests and reasoning. I did, however, spend quite some time at the infantry debussing point at the head of the San Clemente Valley carrying out minor and necessary repairs. These would have had to make the full journey back to Borgo San Lorenzo. That debussing point was a very noisy location. It was in the centre of the gun positions, and therefore a constant target for German artillery and mortars. To me, however, it was not as noisy and dangerous as my past job sleeping on top of the ammunition at Finsbury Park during the early days of the Blitz on London.

Immediately next to and adjoining my workshop at Borgo San Lorenzo was a dilapidated and war-torn cottage. This was occupied by a middle-aged woman who was extremely anxious to offer my Sergeant and me accommodation. Bearing in mind my previous experience in Caldini, I accepted her offer with gratitude. Sergeant Fred Davis and I were thereafter made to feel truly at home.

After about a week, the lady introduced us to a young woman. This, we were told, was Rosilda, her daughter, who had apparently been hiding in the hills while the fighting was going on in the town. She now wanted to return home and her mother had told her it was safe to do so.

By my standards in those days, Rosilda was beautiful, certainly the loveliest Italian girl I had ever seen. She was probably a few years older than I, and quite clearly had her eye on Fred Davis. But Fred was a happily married man who wrote home regularly and, to my knowledge, had no intention of getting involved in anything more than an off-duty drink. He seemed to show no interest in Rosilda, who spoke no English at all, while Fred's knowledge of Italian was extremely limited. In one way, I found his lack of interest very difficult to believe, as she was such a lovely girl. Nevertheless, I tried to point out to Rosilda that Fred was not for her as he was happily married with children. She would have none of it, and just told me that I was too young for her.

My attempt to convince her that I was speaking for Fred and was not interested myself was a waste of time. She only wanted Fred, and was sure that Fred wanted her. I left the matter at that and returned to my work. The next surprise came when Sergeant Davis came to me and asked for a posting to another unit.

'What's the trouble?' I asked him.

'Nothing to do with you,' he replied. 'It's just that Rosilda's a lovely girl, and if I stay here I'll finish up abandoning the wife and kid. I just don't want to get involved.'

I cannot say that I was entirely convinced by Fred Davis's request, but this was an incident that I felt I could use to my personal advantage, and to the advantage of the regiment. My previous efforts to move the workshop to the regimental lines had failed. I would now send Fred Davis up to see if he could find a satisfactory location for the L.A.D. close to the guns, near the debussing point. This was not going to be a very pleasant task, and the Sergeant knew this as well as I. I was therefore surprised when he jumped at my suggestion, and decided to pack his kit and prepare to move out there and then.

The following morning, Sergeant Davis and one of my fitters, Corporal Freddie Ford, moved off. That evening, Rosilda's mother questioned me as to the whereabouts of my Sergeant. I told her that he had gone off to do a job, and would probably be back in two days. I also qualified this by pointing out that some repairs take longer than others.

But Rosilda, who was present during this chat, was no fool. She pointed out that she had seen 'Federico' pack his kit during the night before he left, and that he had never done this before when he had gone off to do a repair job. She then suggested that it was all my fault. I had sent Fred away because she wanted him and not me. Then she said that Fred was not married. He just loved his mother and used to write to her every day. To cap it all, Rosilda then said that she had written to Fred's mother, telling her that they were in love and intended to get married. Being a good Catholic, she had asked Fred's mother for her blessing!

I can only say that I was utterly shocked. This was certainly a most peculiar woman, yet one I could easily have hung up my hat for under different circumstances. Now I felt extremely relieved that I had not been in any way involved with her. I was quite lost for words. This was absolutely outrageous, if it was true.

'Where did you get Fred's mother's address from?' I asked.

'Wait,' Rosilda replied, and walked out of the room. A few minutes later she returned with an envelope that had been well screwed up. She stated that she had walked in on 'Federico' one evening when he was writing to his mother. He had screwed up the envelope and thrown it on the floor because she had disturbed him. The address on the envelope was Fred's home address, and I realised that this young woman was deadly serious in her pursuit of Fred.

I was appalled. 'Leave this to me,' I said, and left the room.

The following morning, I went up to the regimental lines and made contact with Sergeant Davis. Needless to say, he was shocked when I told him what Rosilda had done.

The San Clemente Valley

As far as the Sergeant was concerned, however, this was a matter that he could sort out himself. He qualified this by saying, 'Now you know why I wanted a posting away from Borgo.' I have no idea what happened over this matter. Fred Davis remained with me until the end of the war, and we never discussed the incident again.

It was no surprise to Colonel Greig when I told him that I had found a very suitable location for my Light Aid Detachment in the forward area, subject to his approval. He was well aware of the difficulties we had experienced, and the resulting delays of having to send equipment back to the 'B' Echelon area at Borgo San Lorenzo for repair. I pointed out that we would cut down the delay time by being selective in relation to certain repairs. The Colonel, being a man of few words, said all that he needed to say: 'Carry on, Mr Swain.' That was enough for me.

I moved into a half demolished house with my recovery vehicle and a few fitters. We were on the spot and certainly managed to keep the guns firing for longer periods than before. Remember, some of our vehicles, equipment and guns had been in action almost continuously since our landing in North Africa in March 1943. I have to say, however, that when I first arrived at this new location,

I had some difficulty in getting any sleep. This was the infantry debussing point where we had set up our operation, so it was a noisy location indeed, particularly in the middle of the night, when vehicles full of troops would arrive and be marched off in platoons to their respective positions in the front line.

Thankfully, the war in Italy was coming to an end, and this was something that we had all felt in our bones for some while. After some very hectic barrages, the 19th Field Regiment was suddenly pulled out of the line, and we moved back down through Italy.

The Long Route Home

The drill now was that the Light Aid Detachment followed the last vehicle of the regiment, which was a new experience for me. Exactly how long this journey took I cannot say. Our ageing vehicles were truly falling by the wayside. Consequently, there were times when we did not catch up with the regiment for three or four days. Broken-down vehicles had to be repaired on the road if at all possible, and those that could not be repaired were taken in tow to be repaired when we caught up with the regiment. Some that were too far gone were given to another vehicle to tow until we reached a base workshop.

Generally, when we did catch up with the regiment, they were about to take off again. Then the same routine would be followed, picking up stragglers and repairing what we could on the road.

PART FIVE

The Long Route Home

This was truly a lesson to us all. How grateful we were that we were the victors. It also accounted for the reason why we had found so many burned out, blown up and booby trapped vehicles during our advances in North Africa and in Italy. Had we been the retreating army now, we would have been obliged to do exactly the same thing ourselves.

Christmas 1944, was undoubtedly going to be our last in Italy. The big question was, 'Where next?' It certainly looked like Palestine or Egypt, but we had by this time given up the guessing game in relation to future locations. We were grateful to be alive, in one piece and on the winning side. Wherever it was that the powers that be decided to send us, we would do our job as required. All we wanted was for the war to end, to get home to our loved ones, and restart our lives in civvy street.

Camp 87 Pardes Hanna

Early in January, 1945, we boarded ship at Taranto and sailed for Palestine, now Israel. It was quite an uneventful journey, and we landed at Haifa about three days later. Once ashore, we made our way southward to Pardes Hanna, and took over a ready-made camp referred to as Camp 87, at Hadera. This location would be about halfway between Tel Aviv and Haifa. At Hadera, I shared a large tent with the Regimental Sergeant Major 'Tosh' Hill, with the Sergeants' Mess being about fifty yards away.

The L.A.D. was located within the precincts of the camp. Here I had a large Aldershot Shelter for a workshop, and work commenced almost immediately. There was no urgency about the work as we had experienced before. I had the feeling that, although we were there to tidy up the Regimental equipment, we were going to have a rest. We also did our share of camp guard duty, something unheard of before.

Cairo

The food in the Sergeants' Mess was good; the cook, now having built-in cooking equipment that came with the camp, was able to do us proud. Also, the bar was beautiful, well stocked, and consequently well used. Here we had plenty of opportunity to visit some very important towns and cities.

Early in March, I went to Cairo with Battery Sergeant Major 'Badgie' Johnson of 96 Battery. We boarded the crowded leave train at Haifa, and travelled in a not too comfortable fashion. In Cairo, however, we were allocated a place in the Warrant Officers and Sergeants' Club, and were made very comfortable.

While in Cairo, we visited all of the important sights, including the Sphinx and pyramids at Giza. The sight of those massive stones that had been first hewn to their required shape, then hauled into place by hundreds of slaves, was mind boggling. Here we even went inside one of the pyramids, and viewed the burial chamber. It was quite a trek, bent down and holding a taper that went out from time to time. Then we had to give the guide a tip to get him to relight it

We also visited King Farouk's Palace and viewed his jewels. Truly a king's ransom of wonderful objects of art. We finished up that day with a very memorable trip down the Nile.

Our sojourn in Cairo had to come to an end, and we returned to Camp 87 on 12th March at nine o'clock in the morning. Needless to say, we were very glad to see the back of the very crowded train.

Quite a lot of work had accumulated during my absence, mostly in relation to vehicles and motorcycle. While I had been away there had been some talk about a Divisional Motor Cycle Trial being held and Freddie Ford, an expert motorcyclist himself, had taken in a motorcycle that we felt we would be able to use in this trial.

Camp 87 Pardes Hanna

From Camp 87, we were encouraged to visit many interesting historical places that we would otherwise never have seen. I therefore feel it is only right that I include a brief mention of some of the places I was privileged to go to.

On 19th March, 1945, I went to Jerusalem for the first time, where I visited the Wailing Wall and other interesting places. The King David Hotel seemed to be the centre of attraction here. It was also the army headquarters. Jerusalem was quite an easy day out from Pardes Hanna and I got to know the city quite well. There were plenty of fine eating houses there, apart from the places of historical interest. It certainly looked as if it would now be a regular port of call.

On 8th April, I visited Lake Tiberias, a fascinating sight. The most interesting point of the visit was arriving over the top of a hill and then descending to Tiberias, a wonderful view. I returned to Camp by way of Haifa and had a drink and snack on top of Mount Carmel, overlooking Haifa.

On 14th April, 1945 I had to go to Damascus to rescue one of our broken-down vehicles. This was a most interesting trip. We camped outside Damascus, fixed up the vehicle, then slept overnight in our tents with mosquito nets. I was woken up in the middle of

Battery Sergeant Major Johnson and A.S.M. Swain in Cairo 1945.

the night by the sound of a chameleon eating its way through my mosquito net! We had always encouraged these creatures back in Camp 87 for they kept the insects away. This fellow, however, was hungry and had gnawed quite a hole through the net.

On 7th May, I had the opportunity to visit Bethlehem. It was very interesting, but I was unhappy with the commercialisation of such a place. I found more interest in walking round Jerusalem, and made my way there.

The Divisional Motorcycle Trials took place on Wednesday, 9th May, 1945. Freddie Ford had all of our best wishes. He was the best we had. I even went into this event myself to make up the numbers. I was hopelessly outclassed but enjoyed the attempt. Even Freddie Ford did not get a place, although he finished the course in a good time. The winner was one Harry Eighteen, who I believe was a member of the Divisional Royal Army Service Corps team.

On 24th May, 1945, I left camp with some of the 19th Field Regiment Batteries on something of a 'Showing the Flag' visit to Syria. We drove past Tiberias into Jordan, through Lebanon and into Syria, past Homs, and stopped just outside Hama. Here we stayed for about three nights. The greatest sight was driving along the road past snow-peaked mountains. After the third night, we retraced our journey along the same route, arriving back at Camp 87 at 9.30am.

On 11th June, I visited the Nathanya Leave Camp. This was very well set up, with a nice beach and plenty of swimming. There were also Arab lifeguards. I fancied a swim and went over a lifeguard and asked why the red flag was up, as the sea was flat calm. He told me to just walk into the water up to my knees, no deeper, and feel the undertow. I did this and found it quite difficult to keep my feet from sliding away from under me. I got the message.

The celebrations in the Sergeants' Mess on 15th August, 1945, were great. V.J. Day with a vengeance! It was also my birthday. Celebrations here went on for nearly a week.

On 23rd September, I went to Beirut, an interesting city. It had a Leave Camp as well, which was most enjoyable to visit. Frankly, at this time, I was getting a little fed up with all the places we were visiting. I wanted to get home, as there seemed no future in hanging around in a foreign country. The war was over, and I had made out an application to join the London Metropolitan Police when released from the army. Thus my discharge from the army was my main interest.

I had plenty of work in the L.A.D., but most of the jobs were simple, and rarely very important. We were also kept busy with patrols these days, because of the activities of the Stern Gang, The Irgun Zvei Leumi, and the Hagana. These nationalist organisations were in the forefront of activities to regain the nation status of Israel. We as peace-keepers did not dispute the fact that this would ultimately come about. Our interest was to keep the status quo and leave final decisions on this very touchy matter to the politicians.

For my part I was more interested in the fact that the regimental sports day was to be held on Saturday, 13th October that year. As well as having the normal guard at Camp 87, we had a guard posted around our sports ground. The sports were well attended. I entered for putting the shot, and came second.

It was at the sports meeting that I met some Palestine Police Officers. They were stationed at Jenin, where I had seen a huge jail. After having a pleasant evening in our Mess, they invited Fred Davis and me back to their canteen, and a date was agreed.

Thus in early November, 1945, Fred Davis and I made our way to Jenin. We were entertained in their canteen, and I use the word 'entertained' advisedly. About ten of us were in the bar drinking when a loud series of knocks sounded on the canteen door. I said to my host, 'What the hell was that?'

'That,' he replied, 'is our one and only honorary member.' He left us and opened the door.

In came a donkey. It walked straight up to the bar and tapped it with a front foot. The barman produced a bottle of beer, unscrewed the cork and handed it to a man at the bar. The bottle was placed at the side of the donkey's mouth, and it drank the

Members of the 19th. Field Regt L.A.D., Pades Hanna ~ 1945.

A group of 19th Field Regt. Sergeant's visit the Sphinx and Pyramids of Giza ~ 1945.

With Battery Sergeant Major Johnson in Cairo ~ 1945.

contents. On completion, the donkey once more tapped the bar with a front foot, and another bottle was produced. In all, he consumed four bottles of beer before he headed for the door. Tapping it with a front foot, he virtually asked to be let out. I thought that as the donkey went down the step to the ground outside, it looked somewhat unsteady. I was told that the honorary member usually showed up twice a day, but only if there was someone in the bar.

While in North Africa, I had mentioned in one of my letters to my father that I had used an electric magnet to recover items of German equipment from irrigation wells. The information had apparently interested my father, but he had said nothing about it in his letters at the time. In November, 1945, he wrote to me in Palestine to thank me for the idea, and quoted to me the following story:

As the Divisional Detective Inspector, in charge of 'A' Division of the Metropolitan Police, he had been called in to investigate a suspected murder on Westminster Bridge, where a body had been found. The dead man was a Polish airman named Tadausz Rybczynski. My father would not have it that it was murder, he was convinced it was suicide and that the man had shot himself while leaning against the parapet of the bridge.

To help him with the investigation, my father procured an electric magnet capable of lifting a twenty-pound weight from the river bed. The magnet was taken to the area where my father thought the gun would have dropped into the river, and it was swept with the electric magnet. A .38 revolver was found, and against all odds the airman's own fingerprints were still on the weapon, preserved by the river mud.

Geniefa

In December, 1945, the Regiment moved off to Egypt, to Geniefa, on the banks of the Suez Canal. From here we were able to visit Cairo, and many other interesting places. Later that month, I was able to fit in a long visit to Cairo, complete with accommodation at the Warrant Officers and Sergeants' Club. I knew in my bones that this would be my last visit here. The generally accepted feeling was that we would be released in order of our group numbers, commencing very soon.

Following the leave to Cairo, I set about ensuring that the L.A.D. was in top form. As matters stood, I thought that I would be the first in the L.A.D. to be released. I wanted to make sure that I handed my men and the equipment over in good order. My men were behind me all the way. The result was that even Colonel Greig was complimentary, and that counted for a lot.

On 26th February, 1946, I left camp for Sidi Bish in Alexandria, and stayed at the Transit Camp. On Wednesday 6th March, I left camp at 10.15am, and boarded ship at 4pm later that day. We subsequently set sail for France. We arrived at the port of Toulon during the morning of 11th March, and went straight to a Transit Camp. From there we boarded a train to take us across France, a train crowded with happy servicemen from the army, navy, and air force. The journey was going to be quite long, across France to Dieppe. The big question on everyone's lips was: 'How are they going to feed us?'

The Long Route Home

We stopped at a railway station at 7am the following morning, where bacon and tomatoes, bread and marmalade were served to us all al fresco. Satisfied, we moved on, having had the opportunity to clean out our mess tins. At 2pm we stopped at another station. This time, Egon Ronay would have had a fit. Tins of meat & veg were simmering away in soya stoves on the platform, and we were each served with a very hot tin and a piece of bread. The tins were removed from the open stoves with a coke shovel, and were piping hot. We had to slide them into our mess tins and wait a little. Opening them was another problem, but the contents, once we got the tins open with our army issue knives, were well worth the sometimes scalding effort. The feeding methods on this journey were quite an education - enjoyable, if unusual, and went on in this manner until we arrived at Dieppe at midday on Wednesday, 13th March 1946.

We boarded ship at Dieppe, and were soon steaming across the Channel. As the lighthouse at Beachy Head came into view, a great cheer went up amongst those on board. There was even the hint of a tear in the odd wet eye.

We were, however, suddenly brought back to reality by the ship's loud hailer. A most officious voice announced that we would shortly be landing at the port of Newhaven. Anyone found in possession of Lugers, Barettas, Mausers, souvenir grenades and all manner of other items would be in a lot of trouble. The official voice then changed to a more friendly tone, pointing out that of course many of us had picked up various souvenirs during the course of the campaign we had been through.. It was quite understandable that we wanted to hang them on the walls of our homes and offices. There was then a gap in the speech, and we began to feel that this was not a bad chap after all.

Suddenly, the voice came on again, and this time there was a distinct air of menace in its tone. The Military Police would be searching everyone, irrespective of rank, when we landed. Anyone, and he meant *anyone* found in possession of any of the aforementioned items would be detained. We were reminded that we were not out of the army yet, and the broadcast ended.

I don't think I am overstating the situation, but with the port of Newhaven looming in the not-so-distant distance, an element of panic overtook certain of the homecoming warriors. Certainly our kit would be searched; we'd expected that before the official gave his little talk. It was, however, the sort of warning that only fools would ignore. Clearly, it was taken seriously, for there was an almost immediate move amongst many of those on board to pitch little packages surreptitiously into the sea. It surprised me was that those fairly obvious moves were totally ignored by officials on the ship.

I have often thought since that day that, just a little south of Beachy Head, there must be quite a pile of rusting metal which, given an opportunity, could tell quite a story. As it turned out, few of us were in fact searched at Newhaven, but the piece of applied psychology did have the desired effect.

Once we were off-loaded from the ship, we were very soon gathered together and given travel warrants. These were to get us home, and then take us to the demobilising centre at Aldershot. It was 14th March, 1946 and we were due to be demobilised the following day. I telephoned home to tell my mother that I would be at Victoria Railway Station in about an hour. As I spoke, I realised that she was a little tearful, so I told her not to waste time, particularly if she could contact my father.

I have to say that the subsequent meeting with my parents at Victoria Station is one that I shall never forget. We all had great difficulty finding words to say to each other.

The following morning, I was off to Aldershot. The efficiency and speed of the demobilising process truly amazed me, as it did many of my colleagues that day. It seemed to last for only a very few minutes before I was out of the depot, proudly carrying my 'demob suit' and a few bits and pieces that I had brought home with me in a cardboard box.

I was at last out of the army. I was also very happy, and extremely relieved that it was over so quickly. As I made my way to Norbury, the home that I had not seen for six years, a very strange feeling came over me. A few minutes ago, I had been someone, an Artificer Sergeant Major, a Class One Warrant Officer in the British Army. Now I was a nobody, virtually unemployed, although I did have the Co-operative Wholesale Society to fall back on for a job at the end of my demob leave.

However, I was determined to get into the Police force before that time. As my thoughts rambled on, I had to quietly admit to myself that on this day of all days, the day I had looked forward to for so long, I was feeling well and truly lost.

The happy reunion at Norbury continued, but despite all of the reunions with old friends from pre-war days, I still had the irritating frustration of having to wait to fulfil my one big ambition, to get into the Police Force.

I was thankfully accepted into the Metropolitan Police on 3rd June, 1946, and later started work as a Bobby on the beat in London's West End, after completing my course of instruction at Hendon Training School that year. My dream had at last been fulfilled, and those years in the army stood me in good stead for my future career.